COLD LAKE ANTHOLOGY 2025

Cold Lake Anthology 2025

BURLINGTON WRITERS WORKSHOP

Copyright © 2025 by Burlington Writers Workshop

All rights reserved. No part of this book may be reproduced in any manner without written permission except in the case of brief quotations embodied in critical articles and reviews.

First Printing, 2025

Cover artist: Amber O'Brien Haller

CONTENTS

~~

From the Editors
1

~NANCY C. MOSHER~

Ursine Dreaming
3

~PATIENCE MERRIMAN~

The Gowns
5

~ANDY CARLO~

The Great Hemlock Renaissance of 2026
8

~KIMBERLEY REYNOLDS~

Billie
18

~JEFF BERNSTEIN~

A 21st Century Tanglewood Tale
19

~MASHA HARRIS~

Regrets

21

~KAREN KISH~

An Egyptian Wedding: Burqas and Bikinis

23

~CANDELIN WAHL~

Chihuly's Bowl: A Haibun

29

~TRICIA KNOLL~

Up Above My Head

30

~CAROLINE TSUI~

Returners

32

~AMY HADLEY~

gravity

53

~KIMBERLEY REYNOLDS~

Waiting for My Daughter in the ER

56

~WHIT HUMPHREYS~

Nearer

57

~MIRIAM EDELSON~

Music and the March on Washington, 1963
59

~CANDELIN WAHL~

Hummingbird
65

~WHIT HUMPHREYS~

Snow
66

~LEO GOYETTE~

Louis
68

~MASHA HARRIS~

Overdose
75

~MONICA SHAH~

Waiting for Light
78

~CELI BYER~

Driftwood
79

~CANDELIN WAHL~

Endings: Five Haiku
94

Author biographies - 95
Acknowledgments - 100

FROM THE EDITORS

Dear Reader,

Thank you for supporting Burlington Writers Workshop and *Cold Lake Anthology*. This year's collection features works from 17 artists from four US states and one Canadian province. Dreams, memories, and what might have been are the threads woven throughout.

We open the book with Nancy Mosher's "Ursine Dreaming," a poem from the point of view of a mother bear as she hibernates. As the pages turn, Masha Harris' "Regrets" takes us back to a conversation that never happened, and now never can. Caroline Tsui's "Returners" explores the power of memories--particularly when they are lost. Leo Goyette's "Louis" imagines a lifetime of memories about a brother who didn't exist... or did he? The book ends, fittingly, with Candelin Wahl's "Endings: Five Haiku," which explores how life changes and evolves, and how it's often not possible to understand that something is ending until it's already in the past.

We hope you enjoy the poems, stories, and essays herein, and find ways to celebrate your local writers, poets, photographers, and artists. The anthology would not be possible without creators.

Special thanks to this year's reviewers, who spent many hours reading, discussing, and curating submissions:

Fabian Aruquipa
Joyce Benvenuto
Anne Bower
Jake Dennis
Janet McKeehan-Medina
Bill Pendergraft
Robert Perron
Nelly Shulman

~ Nancy C. Mosher ~

URSINE DREAMING

Suckling blind fur balls in the dark, the She-Bear sleeps.
Does she dream, while she contrives warm milk out of
nothing for her babes,
her cells in slow motion, starving?

Yes, she dreams
slowly,
her claws gripping rocks in icy eddies, as the salmon leap
fat and glistening into her ready mouth.
The crunch of spines, the hot crimson flesh,
the burst of berries on her tongue.

She dreams of the others she has borne and
suckled and nosed out of the den
blinded by sun on snow
wobbling behind her.
They wrestle and forage and one autumn wander
off with no farewell.

She dreams of the musk of the father
Appearing out of nowhere, bearing down on her, his

hot breath on her neck, the opening.

She wakes herself crying out in the endless nights,
Reliving the throb of the festering fishhook in her jaw,
the cub swept down the river,
the bullet that grazed her flank as she nosed a cub
into the cover of the forest.

She dreams and cries and loves and suckles, warm and
faintly stirring,
as the cubs nestle closer and mewl and climb about her belly.
Aware enough, as the sun and moon circle above her and
the northern lights flash and shimmer, beheld by no one but
the wolves,

Asleep enough to know the rhythm of the vast universe, the
thrum of tree roots, sustaining each other and her against
the icy wind.

Asleep enough to remember the buzz that waits in her
drowsy cells for the first taste of budding branches,
of grubs and worms and stolen eggs,
of muscles stretched and pulsing.

Asleep, she knows what it is to grow fat and then be empty,
to nurture and then to let go, to wander and then to rest.

One night she dreams of flying.
She dreams of flying.

~ Patience Merriman ~

THE GOWNS

For my mother

I. Evening

When my mother died my sister gave me her gowns.
They'll fit you, she said.

And they do, but I'll never wear them

They're sexy and slim
They shimmy and purr

But they want to be with my mother
They want to hold her breasts
And hips, they want to dance again
With my father and never will

The best I can promise them
Is a quiet waltz, alone in my bedroom

From time to time

II. Bridal

My wedding dress cost a thousand dollars
But my mother didn't flinch,
Slipping her Macy's card
Across the glass counter
While I looked modestly away.

A thousand dollars for one daughter
For one man, for one day

For all brides are creatures
Of custom and commerce,

Passion and pearls and promises
To come home for Christmas

Today I gave my wedding dress away
To the Hospice Thrift Shop

Thirty-five years in a closet,
Thirty-five years of being faithful

And beautiful, when I wasn't
All that time going slowly out of fashion

I tried on my gown before I added it
To a bag of old shoes

The bride in the mirror looked skeletal:

Older now than my mother was

Before we piled her breast with roses
And left her at the crematorium

I will go to meet my mother soon
Dressed in nothing but spirit we'll dance

In clouds of bone and stardust, practicing moves
Until our guests arrive

~ Andy Carlo ~

THE GREAT HEMLOCK RENAISSANCE OF 2026

It all started with the New Year's Eve storm, 2025. A front blew in from Canada and met a cyclone with snow coming up from the Gulf of Maine. Vermont was where the two of them collided and the snow piled up fast, snow on top of snow on top of everything.

The mills were low on wood just then, from the fall mud season and from what had been a slow start to the winter logging season, so the mills did what mills do when they're low on wood—they raised their hemlock price a little, just to get some logs through the gate. The word went out and everyone got the message.

Just after dawn the next morning, New Year's Day 2026, the loggers headed out to their log jobs. We headed out too—we being the foresters—to mark some timber for them. We all met up on the landing, right at the crack of dawn.

The loggers plowed the snow off the landing while their skidders warmed up, and we stood to the side and ate a snack while our fingers went numb. My truck thermometer said 18 below on the drive in, so by the time the snow was plowed, and the skidders warmed, and the chainsaws gassed, and the chains sharpened, and the snacks eaten, and the loggers were ready to go, we were about ready to go too—or else freeze to death, one or the other. The skidders headed for the trail with their tire chains jangling like old Bobtail, and when they got out in front, we fell in behind with our paint guns in our hands and our snowshoes on our feet.

From the landing, the skidders followed the trail down into the swamp and crossed the stream on the ford. Then they shifted into low gear, blew out some exhaust, and climbed up the other side, headed straight for the mountain. That's where they hit the real snow.

Sometimes the snow was four feet deep on that mountain, but the skidders plowed right through it. Sometimes it was five or six feet deep, but they just kept going. Sometimes they got into a steep part and they'd jig and spin for a minute and barely gain an inch. But then the ice chains caught and up they'd go, to the hemlock.

At first production was slow and the logs were dear, so back at the mill the procurement guys had a meeting. What could be done about it? The head buyer got on the phone with the mill owner to discuss the matter.

"Yup," said the head buyer. "Will do," she said, and she hung up the phone.

The head buyer jotted some numbers down on a piece of paper and rolled her chair over to the office admin's desk. The office admin took the piece of paper and typed the numbers into his computer and then he printed off another piece of paper. Then the procurement guys all gathered round and they studied that second piece of paper pretty carefully. They checked all the numbers, and all the numbers checked out.

"Can we afford to do this?" someone asked. A good question.

"Can we afford not to?" someone else asked. Another good question.

There was discussion as there usually is and then they put it to a vote. And when the results came in, they all agreed. This was what they could do about it—this was what they had to do about it. Everyone looked to the head buyer and the head buyer made the decision.

"Send it!" she said—and the new price sheet went into the fax machine. And when it came out on our end, it showed a few more dollars on the mill-delivered price for good hemlock logs.

And just at that moment, somewhere way off south of Montpelier, the sun broke through clouds. The sunlight streamed through the heavens and poured down onto that resolute capital of Vermont. Observant watchers noted that the light shone most brightly on the very heart of that gritty little city, the brave hamlet of Langdon Street. It skimmed across the snow-laden roofs and creaky old stovepipes of the record store and the architect's office, it lit up the dance studio and the printing shop, it shimmered over the Paperback Trader and it flooded into the forestry office through the grime and dust of our south-facing windows. The sunlight filled that precious old forestry office, that beloved place forever fixed in my memory, and it sparkled and danced over everything in it.

I remember what I saw in the office that day—the papers piled high on the foresters' desks, and the duct-taped tally books and the cruise cards. I remember the paint gun parts and blue-paint-covered screwdrivers and pliers on the work table, and the dusty old books on the shelf that no one ever read. I remember the mud from our boots, tracked into the office and trod into a fine Vermont dust, shimmering like gold all over the floor. I remember how the light shone on the eager faces of the foresters crowded round the fax machine, leaning in to read the price sheet.

And when we saw that new price for Prime hemlock logs—Goodness Gracious, somewhere deep inside we each found our own core of hope!

Out in the woods the snow was so deep that the cutters had to shovel out the stumps to cut the trees. But they were happy to do it—or so they said. They were always saying how happy they were to do a thing when you knew perfectly well that the thing most certainly sucked. But that's just the way loggers are, always happy about something—always as positive as a person can be. At least the money was good and the landings were frozen, and the self-loaders and trailers came in and took the logs to the mills, and the checks arrived mostly on time.

At the mills the logs rolled onto the carriage and they went through the saw one after another. Everyone was in a mad dash to move the logs and get the slabs and sawdust out of the way and tail the boards off the saw. Sometimes the boards got frozen together if they piled up for too long before they went into the kiln, and then somebody had to go and get the loader and jostle them around with the forks to break them apart. But when those hemlock boards came out of the kiln, Boy Oh Boy, they shone like sunlight on a field of hay. It was a beautiful thing to see in the low light of a winter's day (except that it was no more or less beautiful than anything else you'd see on a log job or in a mill yard or in a forestry office in the middle of winter, 2026).

But then a strange thing happened. On Valentine's Day, Channel 3 sent a reporter out to a hemlock mill just like they did every year. But this year, the reporter and the sawyer, they spent quite a lot of time together up there on the log pile. The reporter, he asked her about scaling diameters and log lengths—and the sawyer, she told him about how she has to work around the defects, but how sometimes the defects are the most interesting parts. They talked about the back-and-forth motion of the log carriage—how it goes back and forth and back and forth—and how sometimes it has to slow way down because the log is so big and frozen so hard.

"Nothing wrong with that," she told him.

And for some reason, that phrase caught our attention. And there was something about the way she looked at him when she said it—or at least we thought there was something about the way she looked at him. We all saw it—or at least we thought we saw it. It was on TV.

The neighbors must've seen it too, because next thing you know they came over and knocked and asked: "Oh by the way, we were just wondering: are you cutting wood this winter, and if so, are you, by chance, cutting any hemlock?"

"Good golly," I said, for I'd never heard such a thing before. "Why the interest?"

"Aw I d'know," they replied and looked down at their shoes. "Just something we heard on the news." I guess there must've been something in the air that day, because we exchanged Valentine's cards and a box of chocolates too.

As it turns out, something did happen up there on the log pile, between that reporter and the sawyer. After that story aired, he was seen quite frequently around the mill in the mornings, and she was seen picking him up after the evening news, at the station, in the parking lot, in the mill truck. Rumor had it that they were in love, and the rumor turned out to be true.

The rest of the winter was just like the good old days of forestry. We grew accustomed to the deep snow pretty quick and to the snowshoes, and by Presidents' Day we could mark timber all day long. We carried two gallons of paint on our backs and marked in just T-shirts and never stopped long enough to feel the chill.

We ate all the time. Jana's Cupboard was selling apple fritters again and we ate one in the truck on the way to the job and another mid-morning. Then we had one with lunch and a frozen one in the afternoon. That was about 32,000 calories' worth of apple fritters by the way, but on the way home we bought pizza by the slice from the gas station, one for me and one for the dog. And when we got home we had supper.

On Friday afternoons we went to Julio's for margaritas. Grandes. We argued about Levin and the mowing and what it all meant, and granted there were times when it got a little heated, but I had some valid points I thought. We ended up out on the sidewalk at seven o'clock in the evening and, wouldn't you know it but we ran right into the girls from the architect's office! They were standing there on the sidewalk in a corona of light, a few snowflakes swirling around them. Goddamn it, but they were beautiful! I stepped forward into the light and said, "Hey, babe, me and you..."

(I take that back. I didn't really say that. What I actually said was just "Hey" and they said hello back. And we smiled at them and they smiled back, and it was glorious.) Then somehow we found the truck and made it home without any trouble, and the quarter panel wasn't dented too badly from where I drove it up on the curb by the parking meter by accident.

Spring came and the mud season was like none other. Subarus and Teslas got stuck cockeyed in the middle of Gillette Pond Road and Center Road and on Bert White Hill where the seep is. Nothing could be done about it so they stayed there 'til summer, and even then they had to be yanked out by a skidder. And the sap, which started to run on the afternoon of Town Meeting Day, flowed until the end of April and we boiled and boiled until we ran out of wood. All the syrup graded Fancy that year.

In May, I drove the philistine streets of Montpelier with the windows down, searching for beauty and a place to park the truck. I spied a mother with child over by the Historical Society and thought to myself—but did not say out loud—"Doesn't she look fine, pushing that pram up State Street!"

In the evenings, the mills called. They wanted more hemlock but the loggers had all gone off to Florida. They go every spring. The jobs were shut down for mud season. Canada, Maine, the little mills up by Morrisville, no one could get any fresh-cut hemlock no matter what, so we sold them what we had decked up from the winter, and at good prices too, and we promised more when things firmed up in the summer.

During the summer the grass grew taller than you've ever seen. In the mornings the dew was so thick that you couldn't walk through it but you'd soak your pants right up to the belt. But I waded out into it, and stood there in the mist looking up at the sky like an idiot. All around me hung a halo of vapor and I was right in the middle of it. When the hot disk of the sun broke over the hilltop, it blinded me right in the eye. I reached up, I reached high—I touched the very sky!

When I got to the woods I saw a nice 14-inch hemlock, just a gun-barrel of a tree. There were 24 feet of sawlog in that baby and some very nice pulpwood to boot. I tried out my new Trecoder paint gun and, Boy Oh Boy, that Trecoder worked nice! It painted a bright blue stripe across the stem and another on the stump, and so I marked that tree for harvest. This hemlock here shall be a barn beam, I proclaimed! And that one there, a carving of two clasped hands! And that one there, a kitchen table upon which a mother shall assemble a pie! (Such proclamations helped pass the time while the black flies swarmed, and they kept the mortality away—for a while.)

Late afternoon and I was done for the day, so I headed back to the truck. I dropped my vest and empty paint cans in the bed and sat on the tailgate. I stopped breathing so hard and tried to settle my mind. It was mostly quiet. A hermit thrush sang.

If you ever get a chance to park your truck in a forest in Vermont, with some hemlock and maybe a little sugar maple in it, near the end of a summer day, I encourage you to give this a try: sit on the tailgate, stop breathing so hard and try to settle your mind. Chances are, that's when the hermit thrush'll sing.

You won't see him, but you'll know it's him by his song. It's a four-part song, and it goes like this:

Somewhere in this forest,

Somewhere deep within this prayer,

Somewhere there is someone,

With auburn ribbons in her hair.

... and that's when my own thoughts turned to love.

In the fall of the year it poured rain and we stood under an umbrella and got married. Your parents were there and your grandpa too—John was there and Elizabeth too. How happy we all were—all of them and you and me too.

But it wasn't long after when that Goddamn telephone rang.

The English lady came on and said what she had to say.

She asked if there was someone with me, she asked if I was OK.

I handed you the phone. Time stopped and I looked away.

Sometime later time started up again, but it runs different now—now it runs faster than it should, like it's racing towards the end—and sometimes it skips backwards too. Sometimes it sends me back to that Goddamn phone call as if to jam me through it again—the joy and then the sorrow, the life and then the death, the beginning and then the end—but even so, the hemlock prices pushed higher still.

The rains finally ended and the dry weather came, and on a November weekend we went to Church Street and saw the hemlock desks and armoires and buffets in the furniture showrooms. We ran our fingers along the polished surfaces, the way you run your fingers along the side of a neck and into the smooth place below the ear. It was lovely. We marveled at the swirls of grain around the knots and worried over the price tag, until we both decided: Why not? Why shouldn't we have this thing of beauty in our lives? So we bought it... a desk.

And believe it or not, I'm sitting at it right now—that very same desk.

After all these years, it's been worn smooth by great age and constant use, but it's still solid and strong. It's a substantial thing, a thing you can count on when you can't count on anything else.

This is where we sat to plan this house, where the kids came to watch us work, where we paid all those bills, where we wrote down what to remember about John and Elizabeth and your parents and your Grandpa and everybody else who's died, and everything about 2026 too.

My friends down in Atlanta might say it has patina—and they could be right—but up here we just call it old. When hemlock gets old, it gets about as close to eternity as anything can get. I've heard that a good hemlock desk can last forever.

2026: I've seen quite a few years now, good ones and bad, but for some reason 2026 stands out. Looking back on it, I can't speak to anything else except the hemlock—because that's all I know—but I can tell you this: 2026 was the Goddamn golden age for hemlock. Just cast your memory back there. Remember the log landing at dawn, remember the hermit thrush and his song, remember the rain and the beginnings and the ends, and remember the hemlock tree—forever in the shade but forever straining for the sun. Give thanks. We were so lucky to be alive back then.

~ Kimberley Reynolds ~

BILLIE

The newspapers never got her name right. Always something different about the past. Like a lit cigarette or something that would officially blow out. It all fused into one another like a big picture that never was figured out. She shifted. It wasn't possible to stay ahead of it. The past is like a wardrobe, to be garlanded and then discarded. Nothing permanent here.

In and out of the Harlem joints—Pod's & Jerry's on 133 Street and the Brooklyn Elks Club—just a teenager improvising jazz genius. At Covan's Club—where women swooned at the voice that lifted from the Queen of throats, a warble, a winkle, minks floating, pearls hot against the necks, just a burst of cherry, a woman unlucky in love.

And John Hammond signed her to Brunswick. It was pop tunes, swing, to stoke the jukebox. Still, she could kick with "What a Little Moonlight Could Do." The start of something bigger.

From the small lots of Baltimore and her mother taking "transportation jobs" away from home, it couldn't heal her heart. Replicated in the heroin-suffering haze and just outright dying of heart failure at Frankie Freedom's—a star but never born.

~ Jeff Bernstein ~

A 21ST CENTURY TANGLEWOOD TALE

A WPA mural of a perfect Berkshire
summer has survived for decades
in the dusty meeting room upstairs
at the old Richmond Town Hall.

A man fishes forever off a dock
in a blue, blue pond, unmarred
by civilization, while a woman
sits beside him, rowboat at the ready.

Three huge poplars to the north
frame the water, not a ripple
on its surface. There will be no
darkness that uncomplicated day.

The long-time town administrator,
my dear friend who died during
the pandemic, patrolled the dirt roads
under oak, beech and ash cathedrals.

When I first visited Richmond
one solstice day decades ago
I surveyed the town from a truck bed,
inhaling sweet first-cut hay.

The light stretched so long
I wondered if dusk would ever come.
Last month, a fancy new municipal
complex opened. The old town hall

is up for sale at the bargain
price of $190,000.
If no one calls that ask, it's
coming down, mural and all.

~ Masha Harris ~

REGRETS

I sat on a precarious and uncomfortable couch
As she used the remote to look up
Blue Öyster Cult
Devo
Todd Rundgren
Music I didn't care for, late into the night.
I was exhausted,
But Aunt Mary didn't sleep.
Song after song
Recordings of concerts on YouTube
Stepping up to the TV to point out her younger self in the crowd.

The entire place smelled like Djarums
Which she was kind enough to smoke on the other side of the room.
The smell didn't give me cravings the way I thought it would
But it was hard to sleep when all the smoke came up the vent at night.

At a chain restaurant earlier that evening

A bit of a drive
She had told me the story of why she wasn't welcome at the location closer to her house.
The manager had befriended a squirrel
And Mary thought it best to call animal control.
There was drama. She could never go back.
After dinner she gave me a tour of Charlottesville
At about a million miles an hour
Windows down in a car so old you had to roll them
Stick shift
Elton John blasting on cassette.

She showed me a cross-stitch inspired by an acid trip
Jack and the Beanstalk, an awful and enormous giant
And told me a little about what it was like growing up:
A grown adult
Still visibly terrified of her own father.
And I opened my mouth to say
"Did he ever hurt you?"
I opened my mouth to say
"He hurt me."
I opened my mouth to connect.
But nothing came out
And now she is gone.

~ Karen Kish ~

AN EGYPTIAN WEDDING: BURQAS AND BIKINIS

The minibus won't start. The engine sputters, spurts, and dies. It's 7:00 p.m., a sweaty 90 degrees, and we're seated in gowns and suits, listening to the coughing, stuttering motor.

Sameh and Naglaa's wedding starts at 9:00, and we are key players that include the groom's sister, Sahar.

Undeterred, the six of us sashay out of the van in our finery to push. Neighborhood kids rally around us, a small army of pop-the-clutch hopefuls. The Egyptian driver waits for our brigade's momentum, releases the clutch—and *vroom!*

Clammy with exertion, we pile back in to cool our fancy regalia. Except, in typical Cairo mechanical fashion, the air conditioner is broken.

Our landlords, Hala and Hatem, with their two sons Mohammed and Mahmoud, have already circled our neighborhood's no-people-allowed central garden several times, celebratory horns blaring. Hatem's mother Horara is in another car. Sameh and Satar, Hatem's brother and sister, also live in our six-unit building with Horara. The family occupies three apartments, and we live in one of two flats rented to Westerners. American International School of Egypt colleagues Frank and Barbara live on the top-floor, opposite Hala and Hatem.

On his deathbed, Hatem's father had begged him to promise to oversee his younger brother's completion of college and betrothal. Sameh finished his studies easily. For multiple possible brides, though, Sameh presented the family with gold for the honor of courting their daughter. With each family's denial, the gold was returned, thus ending the liaison before it even began. At age 35, after allegedly dozens of matrimonial overtures, supremely shy Sameh has finally fulfilled both of his father's wishes.

We are supposed to be a boisterous honking caravan all the way downtown to the luxurious Pyramisa Hotel, about 12 miles away. However, Frank and Barbara know well the futility of trying to stay together for more than a block in chaotic Cairo traffic, so they have commandeered Sahar to ride with us as our Arabic interpreter to direct the driver when we inevitably get lost.

High-schooler Joe, Frank and Barbara's son, is entrusted with the safe transport of eight 36-inch, red-and-white striped and beribboned ceremonial candles. As soon as we zoom away, they tumble off the rear seat. One cracks upon impact, so protector Joe scoops all of them into his lap and sits uncomfortably on the floor for the rest of the ride—two hours snarled in gridlock of predictably horrific proportions. Not only are we late, but we've also damaged the matrimonial tapers.

Luckily, bride Naglaa is 20 fashionable minutes late, in spite of being groomed by her hairdresser in the hotel since noon. We are in the marble and gold lobby with a gloriously curved staircase ascending in the middle, waiting to discover how the spectacle of our first Egyptian wedding will unfold after only one month of teaching in Cairo. Luck is on our side: Canadians Frank and Barbara have lived in Cairo for three years and never seen a wedding, but as adopted "family" within our communal apartment building, we are all invited.

The term "wedding" has a different definition in a Muslim context. The official legal papers were signed by the groom and Naglaa's father, without the bride, a few weeks prior at a municipal office. No mosque is involved because a woman and man can't attend together; women are discreetly screened in a corner, separated from the main worship space. So tonight's "wedding" finale is a dazzling party with both of them together for the first time, Naglaa in a satiny bridal gown and Sameh in a classy tuxedo.

Two rows of 20 drummers and tambourine players, in dapper red-and-white formal garb, now encircle those magnificent gilt steps, thrumming and chinkling an opening sonata for the nuptial entrance. Flanking them are two rows of relatives' children, including Joe as a special honor, proffering those flawed but flickering ceremonial candles.

Sameh, beaming, descends the festooned staircase. Next, a herald in a brilliant turban and streaming caftan announces the bride and her father with a piercing, primitive reed horn tattoo. Naglaa and her father gracefully glide down, arm in arm, all beautiful smiles, Naglaa in flowing white with pearl stitching, a gold necklace and sparkling bangles. A shower of rose petals and faux gold coins embraces the couple as the rhythmic drumming and clapping reach an uproarious fever pitch around them. In the lobby, Sameh and Naglaa take turns dancing with family members, a videographer records the affair, the event is broadcast to rooms throughout the hotel, and the splendid celebration begins!

Next is the majestic ascension: a plaintive peasant horn leads the bride and groom up through the musical gauntlet lining the stairs; the children and ritual candles light the way behind them, followed by the guests. Near the banquet hall, uniformed marching attendants—with flaming swords!—encompass the couple. Guests proceed into the hall first so that Sameh and Naglaa can make their grand entrance. As we await them at our table, swirling dry ice smoke, a dozen streaking strobe lights, and blaring Rocky-style music envelop the dimmed room.

The bride and groom are announced, not in Arabic but in surprising English and French, to the strains of "Unchained Melody." They proceed to two raised, gilded thrones near our American-Canadian table. Ceiling-mounted television monitors capture the superimposed, fade in and out, split screen, up-to-the-minute every gesture of the rapturous couple.

We are dazzled by the unexpected pomp and circumstance far exceeding any North American reception. Barbara, wide-eyed, declares, "I bet Elvis will arrive any second!"

The toast is with rose water—no alcohol at a Muslim wedding—with an actual lingering rose palate. We sip water for the rest of the evening, with suspect Nile origins prickling our conscience. Barbara jauntily lifts her glass and solves this parasitic prospect with a toast for our table. "If we go down, we'll all go down together!"

I scan the hall: more than a hundred Egyptians, some veiled in burqas, some not, in formally discreet gowns and suits surround the enthroned, radiant newlyweds sipping their rose water tribute. This is a reception culturally unparalleled in my half century of life. Still, I could *never* have guessed what happens next.

The music wanes and the master of ceremonies airily announces, "Ladies and gentlemen, Mesdames et Messieurs—the Star Girls from Russia!"

From behind a curtain, eight Russian near-children file out—in skimpy bikinis! I'm instantly stunned, dumbstruck. Burqas and bikinis? At a conservative Muslim wedding! *What is going on?*

Tactfully immobile, my eyes covertly slide side to side, surveying the room for reactions. Inscrutable faces betray no nonverbal clues of surprise or acceptance or horror. Across our table, my husband, stoic Sandy, has the best incongruous angle: a solemn, fully-veiled woman seated at the edge of the performance gazing obediently at the juvenile gyrating retinue.

The girls dance their way through various musical routines, smiling with blank eyes, for 45 awkward minutes. I can't seem to breathe. Only during a brief, energetically swiveling belly-dancing interlude does the impassive audience acknowledge the girls—with a raucous burst of enthusiastic clapping. Burqas applauding belly dancing? I glance at Frank and Barbara who look tactfully stricken; teenager Joe is admirably poker-faced. I really need someone to explain this paradoxical turn of events, but I can't ask now.

The gala blithely continues. Men wielding flaming swords march around the wedding cake before it's cut. A buffet appears at midnight and everyone attacks it, ravenous mob style. More singing and dancing—this time by the wedding guests. With the party still in full swing, we leave at 1:00 a.m., luckily find a stretch taxi to accommodate five passengers, and sink into our seats, silently bewildered but too exhausted to process the bizarre spectacle. The taxi delivers us to our beds by 1:30 a.m.—with classes the same morning.

After school, we race upstairs to Frank and Barbara's apartment. Still awed and dazed, we demand: What was *that* all about?

They carefully explain that the scanty show is common for hotel fare, but rare for weddings. Usually the entertainment includes a singer and Egyptian belly dancer (thus the lone strident applause). Either risqué routine would be for Sameh's benefit (and maybe the other male spectators?), a rousing arousal to inspire his wedding night duties. Naglaa, I guess, gets the proverbial cake.

Why bikinis in a burqa-clad ballroom? According to Islam, non-Muslims are condemned to hell, so these nubile Russian infidels can cavort away for the outwardly aloof audience. I speculate about how these once-innocent girls were enticed into this dubious, far-away career, possibly by predatory Russian traffickers.

After only one month in Egypt, we are truly honored to be invited to this sumptuous wedding and to witness our landlords' and their relatives' genuine joy. Everyone was friendly and welcoming to the five of us, the only Westerners in the room.

And yet, there will be other surprising cultural contradictions to decipher while we teach in Egypt.

~ Candelin Wahl ~

CHIHULY'S BOWL: A HAIBUN

On a road trip in Florida, I said yes to transporting fragile artwork halfway across the state. Oversized glass bowl, donated to a Seattle fundraiser by the studio of the famed glassblower Dale Chihuly—its owner retired in Tallahassee. As her health failed, she offered the bowl to my cousin in D.C. With the box buckled in my back seat, I navigated safely to St. Augustine. Another cousin drove the last leg north. The bowl now rests in a Plexiglas case on a velvet cushion—a see-through pink planet etched with latitude lines—sturdier than she looks.

dormant volcano

rim glows gold

draws people to the edge

~ Tricia Knoll ~

UP ABOVE MY HEAD

After Sister Rosetta Tharp

Oh, I hear music in the air
dawn song of thrush
wind flashing seeded grasses

thunder rumbles
head nods count
how far away

my neighbor's TV drones stock prices
to soothe her Newfoundland puppy
when she goes grocery shopping

my news radio crackles
with sky violence and I shuck
corn for chowder rich with cream

while a daughter tells stories
in a church decked out in red geraniums
and high school photos at her mother's memorial

and the happier tales fill
with her mother's dead voice
so I hear my mother in my head

and across a reception room,
gossips catch up on gossip
half-filled with truth in retreat

the hum in my tulip throat
matches the drone of snow tires
on dry pavement

I ask to know the place
that corrals muttered prayers,
offers water and grain

to release their three-beat gallop
into open air,
there must be hope somewhere.

~ Caroline Tsui ~

RETURNERS

Phyllis's lips were cracked. She'd called for water over an hour ago, but the room remained empty. She couldn't even tell if anyone was listening.

A padded metal harness pressed her into a cushioned backboard. The restraint—though comfortable—gave no room for movement.

With a hissing noise, the harness retracted into the backboard. Phyllis stumbled into the room on unsteady legs. She was wearing a clean linen shift, as white as the room.

"Hello, Phyllis!" The wall shifted, opening up for a smiling woman who wheeled a cart into the room. "You are in Blue Point Rehabilitation, a renowned memory facility."

"I—" Phyllis's throat felt dry and scratchy as she choked on her words.

The nurse handed her a half-empty cup of water. Phyllis gulped the water too quickly, water dribbling down her mouth. Nothing had ever tasted so good.

The nurse pressed a stethoscope against Phyllis's chest. Phyllis cleared her throat and found she could speak. "I can't remember anything."

"Don't you worry," the nurse replied. "The procedure can shake you up, but soon you'll be right as rain!"

The nurse unwrapped a small machine and pricked Phyllis's arm.

Phyllis winced. "Why can't I remember anything?"

The nurse stared at a box. "You just returned from the war. You wouldn't want to remember any of that, would you?" The monitor beeped, and she beamed. "Looking good here!"

Phyllis did not feel good.

Something was pushed into her hands.

"This phone will give you instructions about your next steps," the nurse said as she left.

Phyllis looked at the phone. The screen was blank. "Hello?"

A panel slid open from the wall. The phone screen lit up: EXIT.

**

The sky outside Blue Point was pure, continuous gray. Thunder rumbled in the distance and the lighting didn't look quite right. Phyllis wondered if a storm was coming, but a part of her knew it didn't rain anymore.

The phone told her to wait at the bus stop.

Phyllis walked to the large asphalt road and sat at the small shelter. A vehicle flashed past, and dust flew into the air. Phyllis coughed.

It hadn't always been like this, she knew. There used to be plants in place of the dust, and the roads used to be full of vehicles. But now there were no plants and the road was empty. It was some time before a bus arrived for her to board.

*　*　*

The apartment was cramped, with thin, hard carpeting. A bed was tucked into one corner, positioned across from a composting toilet. A closet with four identical outfits was built into the wall. There was no sink and no shower.

A noise brought her attention to the front of the room. A small drawer had sprung open, revealing a cup of water and a dish with soy and potatoes.

Phyllis downed the water, careful not to spill a drop. The food had an awful metallic taste, but Phyllis ate it all anyway.

Her apartment had a small circular window overlooking the street. Phyllis looked at the stormy skies and the lightning that wasn't lightning. She'd been up there, Phyllis knew. There'd been a battle, but every time she reached for a memory it floated further from her grasp.

The window didn't open.

Phyllis fell asleep watching the flashing gray clouds.

*　*　*

The waiting room was empty. Her phone periodically lit up and told her to wait for further guidance. Phyllis shifted uncomfortably. Along with breakfast, the drawer had given her a strange wipe and Phyllis could still feel the chemical film sticking to her skin.

"Hi!" The woman filled Phyllis's frame of vision. Her long blond hair was pinned up, but some strands had escaped, framing her face, "My name is Thea Lee. You must be Phyllis?" She looked at Phyllis, seemingly waiting for a response.

"Oh, um, hello," Phyllis stuttered out.

"It's lovely to meet you, Phyllis. Thank you for your service. How has civilian life been for you?"

It was as if Phyllis had forgotten how to use her voice. "All right, I guess. Still new."

"That makes a lot of sense. But we're happy to have you here, it's a lot easier than what's happening up there!" Thea said.

"Do you know what is going on up there?" Phyllis asked.

Thea gave her a soft smile. "You don't have access to that information yet," she said, not unkindly.

"Do you know when I'll be able to find out?"

Thea took her gently by the arm to lead her forward, "Don't be so eager. The procedure was for your protection."

"Protection? I can't remember anything. Family, friends, career. It's all gone."

Thea shook her head. "Some things are best left forgotten."

The room was filled with cubicles. People silently stared at their screens, typing away on their keypads.

Thea clasped her hands. "We can start with Jonathan's office. He's head of the data department, where you'll work."

With a flourish, Thea opened the door. "Hi, Jonathan!"

Jonathan was a large man who looked thoroughly at ease behind his large wooden desk. He didn't look up from his papers. "Hello love," he said, without emotion.

"This is Phyllis! She joined your team today."

"A pleasure to meet you." He gave a smile that didn't quite meet his eyes.

Phyllis shook her head in an awkward greeting. Her words fled.

Jonathan shifted his attention to Thea. "Hey babe, I have work to do, could you keep the door closed?"

"Oh yes, sorry, of course." Thea guided Phyllis out of the office. "Sorry, Jon. You've told me that before. I don't know why I keep forgetting."

The door shut behind them and Thea smoothed down her skirt. "We've been married for three years. Jonathan knew we were meant to be the second he hired me."

As Thea talked, they walked toward the cubicles and before Phyllis knew it, Thea had sat her down in a small, slightly squeaky chair.

What Phyllis understood from her job was that there were two systems. One system had the numbers, and the other needed the numbers. She used a screen to transfer these numbers between the systems and she had to do a certain amount before she could go home. When Phyllis had proven she could do this successfully, Thea departed, leaving the scent of flowers in her wake.

Phyllis copied the numbers from one system and then typed them up in the other.

Eventually, Thea came back to see if she had any questions. Phyllis searched her mind, but couldn't think of any.

* * *

Everyone at the office liked Thea. Thea always smiled when you greeted her and remembered your name. She asked about your day and wore nice clothes, the types that weren't sold anymore in the stores. Thea ate her lunch in the break room, surrounded by people who talked and laughed about the day.

Phyllis wished her coworkers would pay her half as much attention. She attempted to make small talk but struggled to remember details about their lives. In response to her fumbled attempts they would offer brief smiles before quickly excusing themselves. They would flatly ignore her if she asked direct questions about the war, walking away without a word. After a few weeks, Phyllis realized that if she didn't go out of her way, she could spend a whole day not speaking to anyone at all.

And then one morning, she found a piece of cardstock on her desk. The paper was thick, but soft, with precise lettering on it.

You're Invited! it said.

Thea was throwing Jonathan a birthday party. The whole office was invited. Phyllis felt a tingle of pleased anxiety. Parties had become increasingly rare as resources and curfews grew ever stricter.

Her cubicle was designed to be soundproof, but she still heard whispers about outfits and brandy and jewelry.

***

Phyllis paused in front of the two-story house. Houses weren't built anymore, but here was a whole block of them, standing even and tall against a smooth dark road. Her phone was silent in her hands, and Phyllis felt a beat of anxiety as she looked at the blank screen. Having nothing to follow seemed wrong.

But she was already there, so Phyllis knocked on the door.

Thea greeted her with a big smile. Her blond hair was curled and she was wearing a soft pink dress.

"Phyllis!" she said, delighted. It was like Phyllis was the one person she truly wanted to see.

Phyllis could do nothing but smile back. "Sorry if I'm a bit early."

"Nonsense, come in." Thea pulled her inside.

Thea's house had an open living room with a large sofa and matching armchairs. Wooden floors creaked underneath their feet and shelves lined the walls, filled with technology and books and games.

"It's huge," Phyllis remarked.

Thea smiled. "We inherited from Jonathan's family." She took Phyllis's hand. "Come. Take the grand tour."

Jonathan reclined on the couch, watching one of the screens. He did not acknowledge Phyllis as Thea showed her the kitchen and the dining room.

When Phyllis asked to see the upstairs, Thea obliged her. Each of the bedrooms was bigger than her whole apartment. Thea seemed pleased by her wonder, but what truly interested Phyllis was Jonathan's study next to the stairwell. And as Phyllis glanced through it, committing it to memory, Thea talked.

She talked about how she was worried that people wouldn't have a good time. And she especially hoped that people ate dinner beforehand because rations had been growing even more scarce and there might not be enough snacks for everyone.

Phyllis could listen to Thea talk for hours about anything and by the time the first guests arrived Phyllis had been swept up in her mood, a certain concern that things would not be perfect.

But there was no reason to be worried. Every single person from the office had shown up. As the house filled up, Thea was whisked away again and again until she no longer returned.

Phyllis floated around from room to room, listening for any discussion of the conflict. There were always hints about it in conversations. Her coworkers spoke with longing about the siblings who were no longer with them and complained about the rations that only grew tighter. There was widespread fear about the upcoming draft. But nobody spoke about the conflict directly enough for Phyllis to gain any real understanding of what was going on.

* * *

Phyllis double-checked the room before quickly ascending the stairs. The sounds of the late-stayers in the kitchen faded behind her as she slipped into Jonathan's study.

The screen was locked. Instead, Phyllis rifled through the large stacks of paper on the desk, squinting to see through the dim hallway light.

Most pages were redacted, the information withheld by thick stripes of black marker. There were some bills related to some spacecraft machinery. Files and files and files with information she didn't need or didn't understand. Phyllis flicked through them quickly, listening for anyone who might disturb her.

Attached to one of the files was a picture. She flipped it over carelessly and paused. Humanity hadn't yet formed the cloud cover to hide the creature, and it filled the sky, dimming the sun to a pale, weak circle. Its proboscis plunged into the ocean, pulling thousands of gallons of water up every second.

Humanity had nicknamed the creature Oizys.

Phyllis stared at the picture and felt herself return to the war, wearing dark camouflage and buzzed hair like the rest of her team. Everything in this world was metal and hard and functional. Oizys's siphon was silent in space and Phyllis followed the thundering column of water to see the parched yellow Earth below.

The biotech machine was designed to bind to Oizys's proboscis and divert water without detection. As her platoon guided the machine forward, the voice in their helmet spoke. "Steady," it commanded her platoon. "Submerge it slowly. Too fast, and Oizys may notice."

They'd been briefed on this a dozen times and drilled for longer. Phyllis breathed as the machine entered the proboscis easily. As they held it steady, a small green light flashed, but no water entered the pump. The machine began to shiver.

"It is vibrating. Is this normal?" she asked.

Silence in the team's headsets. The tremors increased and no water exited the machine.

"I repeat, there is vibration. Should we abort the mission?"

No response. Her team could not leave until explicit permission was given. Phyllis tightened her grip as the machine began to shake.

"You need to back away," the voice said, but the advice came too late, and the machine flung itself toward them.

Pain lanced through her hip and Phyllis heard her team screaming as they were thrown backward from the impact. She fought her instinct to look where she was falling and snapped her eyes shut.

When Oizys first appeared in the sky, entire cities stared upward and turned mad.

Phyllis landed on her back and grunted as pain shot through her hip. The screams in her headset cut off abruptly as comms were isolated. Phyllis lay there and panted, tightly closing her eyes.

It was silent and dark. Her hip throbbed. She felt Oizys's presence above her. Watching.

Waiting. She'd heard the creature had quadrupled in size as it moved around the world. No water molecule seemed able to resist Oizys's call, tearing away from every lake and water treatment plant to join the siphon.

Phyllis wanted to look up, to see and absorb Oizys. The headgear, which usually worked to keep her eyes locked forward, now prevented her from twisting her head to the side. She wondered how long it had been. Surely just a few minutes, but it felt longer. Phyllis had the passing thought that maybe her commanders intended to leave her.

Why was she squeezing her eyes closed? Phyllis couldn't remember. If she was going to find her way back inside the spacecraft, she needed to see.

Phyllis opened her eyes to see the elongated purple creature. It filled her vision until she could see and hear nothing else. And then she was screaming, and screaming, and screaming.

The intensity of her heartbeat brought her back to Jonathan's study. She was choking. Phyllis looked away from the picture and tried to suck air into her lungs, but all she accomplished were useless gasping noises. She let the picture flutter to the floor. Phyllis put her head between her legs and began to breathe. In and out. In and out, focusing on every breath.

At the periphery of her consciousness, Phyllis heard footsteps coming up the stairs. The sound seemed inconsequential at first. Nothing mattered except the Oizys blotting out the sky.

Jonathan's voice snapped her out of it. He was angry. "Why the hell would you think that was acceptable?"

"You've had too much to drink." Thea's voice was shaking.

"That was my stash, you had no right—no fucking right—to take it."

Thea's voice pleaded with him. "You need to drink some water. It's not like—"

Thea was cut off and Phyllis heard the unmistakable sound of a fist colliding with flesh. Phyllis froze.

"You fucking bitch."

Phyllis hurtled out from behind the door. Thea was crouched low, and Jonathan was standing over her, about to strike again. Seeing Phyllis made him lower his hand in surprise.

"What are you doing here?"

Phyllis stood next to Thea. "You need to stop."

"I don't need to do anything." Jonathan was drawing closer to her, invading her space. "This is my house, and this is my wife."

Phyllis could feel the malice emanating from him. She met his gaze.

"I think you should say goodbye to your guests downstairs. I would hate for them to hear anything," Phyllis remarked.

Jonathan glared at her, and for a second Phyllis was sure he'd strike at her too. Part of her wanted him to. The pain would be a welcome distraction.

"Bitch," he spat out, before retreating down the staircase.

Phyllis watched him leave, on guard until he was out of sight. Behind her, she heard Thea's gasping, shuddering breaths, and the bathroom door opening. Thea was standing at the sink, tears dripping down her face.

Phyllis moved forward to pat her on the back. Thea's thin figure was shaking as she tried to cry silently. A sob escaped, tearing through the air.

"I'm sorry," Thea whimpered.

"For what?" Phyllis asked, "Are you okay?"

"Yes," Thea sputtered. "It's just that... he was drinking so much, and he wouldn't stop and I—" She was crying again.

"You did the right thing," Phyllis said.

Thea sobbed harder, wrapping her arms around Phyllis. "Thank you for saying that." There was a red mark on her cheek, visible even in the dim light.

"Do you need to visit a medical facility?" Phyllis asked.

Thea shook her head.

"Are you sure? I think that it might be important for you—"

"I'm not going," Thea snapped at her. Phyllis closed her mouth. She'd never heard Thea sound like that before.

"Okay," Phyllis replied. "Do you need a place to sleep tonight?"

Thea sank her face into her hands. Then she nodded.

"All right," Phyllis said, extending her hand. "Let's go."

They descended the stairs quietly. Soft sounds of movement and gossip came from the kitchen, but no one tried to stop them as they slipped into the night.

Phyllis's apartment looked smaller and greyer after the splendor of the party. Phyllis was worried Thea would think it was drab, but Thea walked straight to the bed and lay down. Phyllis took the floor for the night, replaying her memory of the siphon. It took up thousands of gallons of water every second. Phyllis thought of all the training and drills they'd performed. All useless in the face of real adversity.

***

Phyllis's eyes ached when the phone woke her. She'd slept fitfully, waking often to dreams she couldn't remember. Thea was lying on the bed, huddled around her phone. She was watching those shows that were too expensive for Phyllis.

Thea looked up at Phyllis with red-rimmed eyes. "I helped myself to your closet. I hope you don't mind."

"No, all good."

The drawer sprung open, revealing breakfast. Phyllis brought the dish over to the bed. Thea took a bite of the soy protein and winced. "This is awful."

Phyllis wished she had something better to offer. "Sorry, I know it's bad."

"Oh, gosh, no it's fine. Thank you for feeding me." But Thea put the fork down anyway. There was an awkward silence as Phyllis tried to think of something to say.

"Do you think you'll go to work today?" Phyllis asked.

Thea shook her head. "I don't want to see Jonathan. You should go though. Keep up pretenses."

"Okay." Phyllis looked at her. Thea's cheek was red and slightly inflamed. "Has Jonathan done this before?"

"Hit me?" Thea asked. "No. At least, I don't think so."

"You should leave him."

Thea scoffed, "And go where? What little money I make goes into his bank account. My family is dead. I was on the cusp of enlisting when he hired me."

"You could always stay with me," Phyllis offered.

"You're so sweet," Thea said. "I'll think about it."

It felt distinctly like a soft no, and Phyllis felt the shame creep to her cheeks. Her ugly apartment was barely big enough for one person. Thea wouldn't want to live with her.

They shared the meal silently, watching the small people on the screen argue about which clothes were superior.

* * *

Jonathan's office was empty when Phyllis sat down in her cubicle. Perhaps, like Thea, he'd decided not to attend work. Phyllis booted up her screens, determined to finish her data quickly.

Phyllis heard the door open and Jonathan walked through. His eyes flicked toward Phyllis and Phyllis quietly returned his gaze. She wondered if he would ask after Thea, or try to finish their argument from last night.

Instead, Jonathan pulled his teeth back in a strange echo of a smile and went inside his office, closing the door behind him.

Phyllis's eyes stung as she returned to her data.

Later in the day, Phyllis heard one of her coworkers ask after Thea.

"She's not feeling well," Jonathan replied.

"Oh, again? I'm sorry to hear that. Tell her I hope she gets well soon. It was such a fun party."

* * *

Phyllis came home to find Thea with different foods spread across the table. There were different cheeses, breads, and even meat. And best of all, dozens of canned waters.

"Hey, Phyllis," Thea's voice was dim. "I've bought some food, do you want some?"

Phyllis stared at the foodstuffs in wonder.

"Come eat!" Thea said. "It's for us."

Phyllis grabbed a can of water and drank her fill. It tasted fresh and clean.

"This is amazing."

"This stuff? You should have seen the food and drink that we had a year ago. The grocery shelves were full, and you could pick out three separate snacks per week."

Phyllis stuffed some bread in her mouth. "Thank you for getting all this. How do you have the money for this stuff?"

Thea picked apart a roll with her hands. "Well, Jonathan makes a lot, and spending his money is the least I can do to thank you for sharing your space with me. I can take the floor tonight if you want."

"No, it's okay," Phyllis replied. "The floor is more comfortable than it looks."

"I'm sure that's not true. We'll share the bed. There's more than enough room."

There wasn't, but when nighttime came, Phyllis lay down beside her anyway. Thea must have found a way to shower. She smelled fresh and clean, not like the acrid wipes provided. Phyllis was conscious of Thea as they stared out the window together, watching the flashing clouds.

"I remember what's out there," Phyllis said softly.

Thea looked toward her. "I thought they erased your memory."

"I went through your husband's files. Found a picture of it."

"Oh." Thea gave a weak laugh. "I wondered why you were upstairs. Is Oizys as scary as everyone says?"

Looking upward, Phyllis swore she could see a flash of purple. "Worse."

Thea paused. "Do you think we're going to win?"

Phyllis thought back to the terrifying, unstoppable siphon of water. "No."

Thea shivered and turned over, away from Phyllis. "I've got a doctor's appointment tomorrow. Would you take me there?"

"Of course." Phyllis was glad Thea was receiving help.

* * *

When Thea came through the hospital door, she greeted Phyllis with a bright smile.

"Your name is Phyllis, right? How has civilian life been for you?"

"I guess it's been fine." Phyllis was confused. "How are you feeling?"

"So much better," Thea chirped.

"What did the doctor say about your cheek?"

Thea touched the mark. "Oh that? I just tripped. I can be clumsy sometimes, especially if I drink."

"What are you talking about? That's from when Jonathan hit you."

"Hit me?" Thea laughed. "No. Jonathan loves me. I just overdid it at the party."

Phyllis stared at Thea's vacant eyes and came to a realization. "You got a memory procedure done."

Thea nodded. "That makes sense."

"Why would you do that?" Phyllis asked.

Thea ignored her question. "You must be here to help me get home."

Phyllis had hoped she could guide Thea back to the apartment, but Thea simply followed her phone to Jonathan's house, cheerfully narrating the entire time.

"All right, well I had a lovely walk. I'll see you at work tomorrow!" Thea said, turning toward the house.

"Thea. I..." Phyllis was at a loss for words as Thea beamed at her. "Are you okay?"

"I'm amazing, Phyllis." And with one last smile, Thea walked into the house, leaving Phyllis to her silence.

* * *

In the office, Thea had suddenly decided they were best friends. She made several attempts to engage Phyllis in conversation, but Phyllis shut her out with monotone one-word replies. Phyllis wasn't about to pretend like nothing happened.

Instead, Phyllis watched Thea from afar, searching for signs of abuse. There were none. Thea was back to conversation-filled lunches and holding hands with Jonathan. Phyllis craved her happiness.

Going back to her apartment every day was a terror. Nightmares plague her sleep, and she often woke more tired than when she fell asleep. Left alone to her thoughts. Phyllis paced the room. It had always been quiet, but now the unrelenting silence grating on her. Phyllis could feel Oizys's presence as her thoughts drifted. Sometimes she swore she caught a glimpse of something purple, but when she went to investigate, there was nothing there.

* * *

"Could I have your attention?" Jonathan stood at the front of the room, Thea perfectly fitted into his arms. As everyone in the office turned to look at them, Jonathan smiled. Phyllis thought he looked predatory.

"I am happy to announce that after three years of applying, Thea and I have been allotted a chance to try for a baby!"

Phyllis froze in horror as the office began to clap. Many of her coworkers rose to congratulate the happy couple.

Phyllis shook her head and continued to work. Later, she found Thea in the break room.

"Big news about you and Jonathan."

Thea smiled. "We're really excited."

"And Jonathan is treating you okay?" Phyllis asked cautiously.

"Of course!" Thea chirped. "We've never been better."

Phyllis looked at Thea. "So you're happy?"

Thea beamed. "I've never been happier."

Phyllis nodded before going to schedule an appointment with Blue Point.

***

Phyllis hummed a tune as she took the bus to work. Although the job was an endless sequence of numbers, Phyllis found she was looking forward to the day. Thea had sent her a song last night, and it would be a fun discussion topic.

But when she entered the office, Thea's desk was empty. That was strange. Thea hadn't mentioned she'd be out today.

After Phyllis erased her memory, Thea was the first person Phyllis met from the office. Thea laughed as she showed Phyllis around, patiently explaining everything, even though apparently this was the second time they'd done the tour.

Phyllis pulled out her phone and sent Thea a message. No response came.

Phyllis went to knock on Jonathan's office door.

"Not today," a gruff voice said.

Phyllis opened the door anyway. "I noticed Thea hasn't been in today, do you know where she is?"

"I was about to ask you the same," Jonathan said. "She was gone when I woke up. I thought she might have come into work early, but apparently not."

"She isn't answering her phone," Phyllis said.

"I know," Jonathan said. "I'm beginning to worry."

Jonathan looked worried. He had dark circles underneath his eyes, and his tie, usually immaculate, was crooked.

Phyllis felt a growing concern. This wasn't like Thea at all.

"Should we call someone?"

"I'm going to give it a few hours," Jonathan said. "Sometimes she loses track of time."

Phyllis gave a nod and closed the door. Hopefully, Thea would be back soon and all this worry would be for nothing.

***

The next day Phyllis was summoned to the conference room.

"Hello, Phyllis. My name is Officer Simmons. I'm here to ask you a few questions about Thea Lee."

Phyllis felt a pit in her stomach. "She still hasn't been found?"

"Not yet. I'm going to do my best to find her." Officer Simmons closed the door and pulled out a small notepad. "Did Thea have any enemies or issues with anyone?"

If Phyllis had felt less nervous she would have laughed. "Thea? No. She's always kind and helpful."

"Then jealousy perhaps? Someone could be jealous of her?"

Phyllis shrugged. "Nobody comes to mind."

"How was her relationship with Jonathan?"

"They were planning a family together," Phyllis said. "Thea loves him quite a bit."

"Nine times out of ten it's the husband," Officer Simmons said, putting down his notepad and staring at her. "Is there any chance Jonathan might be involved in this? You can speak freely."

Phyllis shook her head. "Jonathan is a little gruff, but he dotes on Thea, everyone sees it. They were so excited to start a family."

Officer Simmons nodded. "Thank you for your time."

As Phyllis returned to her seat, she felt Jonathan's gaze on her. Phyllis gave him a small smile, but he turned into his office, shutting the door behind him.

* * *

The detective took interviews for about a week, before fading away. Whispers around the office said he'd been unable to find any information. His current theory was that Thea was just a bored housewife who left to find more adventure. Maybe she'd enlisted under a false name. But that theory rubbed Phyllis the wrong way. Thea wasn't the type to pick up and leave.

Jonathan grieved. He came in late, with dark circles under his eyes, and was distracted in meetings. Some people in the office banded together to make him casseroles so he would have enough to eat.

Phyllis continued working. She went into the office, ate the same metallic food, and waited in vain for water. Sometimes she had an interesting idea, but her finger hesitated when she reached for her phone, not sure who she would tell.

* * *

When the office door opened, Phyllis's eyes turned in hope. But Jonathan, not Thea, walked through, a young brunette trailing behind him. She was pretty, with long braids. Phyllis watched as Jonathan led her around, explaining how the office worked in soft tones. Phyllis didn't like how close they were. As Jonathan departed, the woman sat down in Thea's chair.

Phyllis stared at her harshly. That was Thea's chair, and the newcomer had no right to it.

Phyllis entered Jonathan's office without knocking. "How are you feeling about Thea?"

She had been hoping to shock him into anger, but Jonathan only looked up at her blankly. "Who's Thea?"

Phyllis blinked. "Your wife," she reminded him slowly.

Jonathan shook his head. "I've never had a wife."

Phyllis stared at him.

"Go back to work, Phyllis."

Phyllis walked out of his office and out the door. She'd seen the red advertisements all around the city. They bragged about the glory and money that came from joining the cause. It seemed far more worthwhile than transferring numbers all day. The processing station was only a short bus ride away.

"Hello again! What can I do for you?" The lady at the front desk greeted her.

"I'm here to enlist."

"We're always grateful for your service," she said, typing on her screen. "Phyllis Corinth?"

Phyllis nodded.

"Another returner." The lady gave her a badge. "They always come back."

~ Amy Hadley ~

GRAVITY

I'll never forget your face as you were leaving,
your hair still mussed & hanging in your eyes from our ride in
   the old T-bird convertible.
how you crossed the tarmac, glancing back over your shoulder.
the love & fear in your eyes.
you never did like flying. said you *"just don't get it, the defying of
   gravity."*

the old T-Bird gave up the ghost that same night as I pulled into
   the driveway.
she's been under canvas in the old barn for a while now
untouched since that day.
I'm not sure it's been long enough.
but...
yesterday I took a deep breath & uncovered her in one fell
   swoop, disturbing a layer of dust.
& then, when the air cleared, I opened the trunk.
I'd forgotten how much stuff one can cram into 22 cubic feet.
remember those flip-flops, the flimsy purple ones you found at
   the five & dime

insisting, in your best French accent, that *"zay were all zee rage back in Paree"*?
"Say what?" I remember answering, *"Paris Kentucky maybe."*
I slipped one on for old times' sake and it pretty much disintegrated. I laughed.
until I cried.
the red-plastic sand bucket still had shells in it, including that odd circular one you slipped on my finger, declaring your everlasting love.
& of course, there was the ratty old blanket, even rattier now.
how many hours did we while away stargazing, wrapped up in that old thing,
tucked away in the cradle of the dunes, listening to the music of the surf
like we were the only two people on earth...
I can still taste the sweet muscadine wine. feel time standing still.
& oh!
the stars, millions of them, shimmering. *"each one is someone's soul, shining its light,"*
you said *"one day we'll be up there, shining on..."*
how many wishes did we make?
"I'd like to learn how to defy gravity," you told me on that last night.
"Well," I replied. *"You could find a place in outer space, float blissfully amongst the stars,*
watch over me from afar...or...
you could just kiss me."
& that's what you did.

you should be back in the city now, surrounded by towering
   skyscrapers, neon and noise.
when I got the call...what are the odds, I thought, that your
   plane would be one of the ill-fated four.
that gravity would pull you from the sky...
I went to that field in Pennsylvania last month
sat there until well after dark thinking about you.
& I wished upon a star.

shine on, my love.
shine on.

~ Kimberley Reynolds ~

WAITING FOR MY DAUGHTER IN THE ER

Your first thought is will she go on living
And then your head fills with minutiae,
Will the food rot in the fridge
Does the door handle turn left or right?

But we are here now, scooped in with the swirl of humanity—
Now we are here wanting for the specific pinprick of an answer.
This could be every moment or no moment—
It is the only moment

The moment of truth
In abject honesty and hope,
You've never wanted so much truth in your life.

It is an illusion—the streak of light across the sky
Your husband haggard in the fluorescence
But it will come down to this: She is your daughter
And you will go on living.

~ Whit Humphreys ~

NEARER

Nearer my god I may be,
but 'til now we had met infrequently,
and not asked questions of each other.
So, I was puzzled when the god in me
got lonely and sought me out.
The gold leaf brushed over crimson leaves,
the autumn sun dusted on the maple trees...
That flare of the holy in the backyard asked:
are you ready for such a terrible beauty?

Which made me look around for something to do.
Something we could do together, perhaps.
Stack wood, weed-whack, mow the grass.
Or we could just sit and listen, so that in time
we might write poems together,
I and my new numinous friend.

I asked, as one might when accompanying a god,
if I would outlive my cat, or if this is my last pick-up truck
holding its final cord of wood.
The answer was *go rake maple leaves*

as if your life depends on it,
I'll be on the porch watching.
So I raked the leaves which earlier
had stunned me with their fire and light,
over which now a new beauty had fallen.

~ Miriam Edelson ~

MUSIC AND THE MARCH ON WASHINGTON, 1963

Music accompanied a lot of activities in my childhood home on Long Island. Jazz, folk and classical were among the genres my parents enjoyed most. In an earlier time, my dad had worked as a radio disc jockey at what he called a "serious" music station in Newark, New Jersey, broadcasting classical music and jazz to New York City residents across the Hudson River. He spun records and added his own historical and social commentary to create the programs. In our home, we were treated to these same kinds of stories as we listened to jazz greats, classical music and folk singers. Protest music was also high on the agenda, including Woody Guthrie, Pete Seeger and later, Bob Dylan and Joan Baez. It was energizing to listen to these singers and to learn the lyrics to their songs. Absolute poetry!

He also favored Black singers, many of whom were prominent during the Civil Rights Movement. Paul Robeson, Nina Simone, Harry Belafonte and Johnny Mathis were frequent choices on my dad's "top ten" list. My father would plant himself in our living room, crooning along to Johnny Mathis. I would often join him, my clenched fist a pretend microphone, as I tried to get the lyrics and tune just right.

So when my dad announced one night at the dinner table in August 1963 that he was going to join the March on Washington for Jobs and Freedom, we were not surprised. It seemed a logical step for a political man who was committed to racial equality. Our family had marched in civil rights rallies and gathered to listen to speeches from significant Black leaders. At one march when I was three or four years old, I had felt scared by the press of people, most of whom were Black. And I felt guilty for feeling scared, because I knew we were doing something important. When my dad told us he would go to Washington, I got it. I was only six years old, but we'd been raised to cherish such values.

Nonetheless, when it came time for him to go, I pleaded with him to take me along. His worn brown leather catalogue case with tall flaps on the sides and top closure, the piece he took on his frequent business trips, was by the door. Although I could barely fit in it as comfortably as I had a couple of years earlier, I staged a sit-in (literally) to stop him from leaving without me. I was unsuccessful and he left to catch a bus hired by one of the union or civil rights organizations in which he was active.

I was heartbroken. It would have been August 28, 1963, the March on Washington, and Dr. Martin Luther King made his iconic "I have a dream" speech the next day. When my father came home, he regaled us with stories about the March and Dr. King's wonderful speech. He said that he was deeply moved by the experience.

The movement to build toward the March was energized by the music we listened to in my home. In fact, music was an essential part of the Civil Rights Movement. It was a powerful and transformative force, serving as both a means of expression and a tool for mobilization. It provided a shared language for activists, fostering a sense of community and shared purpose.

Benefit concerts known as "Salute to Freedom" were mounted across the country to raise funds for the March. Such concerts were held in Birmingham, Alabama, as well as Chicago, New York City, San Francisco and Detroit. More than 150,000 people attended, both Black and white supporters.

Birmingham had seen extreme racial tension in May 1963. The city was one of the most segregated in the South, with entrenched racial divisions in all aspects of life, including schools, employment and public facilities. That racial strain—including terrible lynchings—was a focal point of the Civil Rights Movement and a turning point in the fight against segregation and racial injustice in the Jim Crow South. In early 1963, the Southern Christian Leadership Conference (SCLC) and the Alabama Christian Movement for Human Rights (ACMHR) launched a series of nonviolent protests and civil disobedience actions designed to provoke a response and draw national attention to the injustices in Birmingham and other places. The campaign was led by Martin Luther King Jr., along with others. The son of my parents' close friends, a university student, participated in Freedom Summer in 1964, going south to Mississippi to register Black voters. It was a dangerous time during which three students were killed by the Ku Klux Klan, drawing national attention to the risks faced by civil rights activists.

Activists also organized sit-ins at segregated lunch counters, as well as marches and boycotts of downtown businesses.

These actions aimed to disrupt the status quo and pressure local businesses and the city government to desegregate. The movement took a dramatic turn that May with the involvement of young people in what became known as the Children's Crusade. Thousands of Black students skipped school to participate in peaceful marches. The use of children was strategic, as it aimed to elicit a more sympathetic response from the public and media.

The police ordered the use of their dogs and high-pressure fire hoses against the young demonstrators. Images and footage of children being attacked by dogs and knocked down by powerful streams of water shocked the nation and drew widespread condemnation. The brutality highlighted the extent of racial injustice in Birmingham and garnered significant media attention.

The Birmingham campaign of 1963 is remembered as a pivotal moment in the Civil Rights Movement. We never learned about this in school. The campaign showcased the power of nonviolent protest, the resilience of the Black community, and the importance of media coverage in exposing injustice. The courage of the demonstrators, particularly the children, and the leadership of figures like Martin Luther King Jr. left an indelible mark on the struggle for civil rights and equality in America. What transpired in Birmingham is considered instrumental to the passing of the national Civil Rights Act the following year.

Later in 1963, a coalition of national civil rights organizations began planning a benefit concert for August 5 in Birmingham. It was one of the ways funds were raised to support the March on Washington. The organizations involved included the National Association for the Advancement of Colored People (NAACP) and the Congress of Racial Equality (CORE), as well as Clarence B. Jones, one of Dr. King's closest advisors and speech writer. The concert was spearheaded by comedian Joey Adams, a Jew, who was president of the American Guild of Variety Artists, a part of the AFL-CIO (the largest federation of unions in the country). The concert was planned as the first integrated event of its kind in Birmingham.

Ray Charles; Nina Simone; Johnny Mathis; The Shirelles; The Staple Singers; Peter, Paul and Mary; Odetta; Harry Belafonte; Mahalia Jackson; Joan Baez and Bob Dylan; author James Baldwin and comedian Dick Gregory were among the many artists who participated in the Salute to Freedom concert. Dr. King watched intently from the side of the stage.

My father never spoke about these spectacular performances. Certainly, we listened to these artists on our chestnut Magnavox record player at home. But music was not the only glue bonding me to my dad. In addition to his job as a disc jockey in the late 1940's, he was a radio announcer for a program called "Labor News and Views." He did political education for the United Electrical Workers and the radio program was part of the attempt by progressive unions to build a united front after World War II. Until he was blacklisted, my father interviewed leaders and rank-and-file members of various unions about their challenges, failures and victories. All of this occurred long before I was born.

My dad brought back a small red and black banner as a token from the March on Washington. I inherited it when he died. I had it framed and hung it in my union office, where my job was to defend the human rights of union members. I spent 30 years working for unions in different capacities. It seemed quite fitting, the circle unbroken, between my father's dedication to the cause and my own life's work. Music and civil rights had captured both of our imaginations and influenced our life choices. He didn't take me to Washington in 1963, but in an enduring fashion, I am still living out the March's legacy.

~ Candelin Wahl ~

HUMMINGBIRD

for Mia Elizabeth

What's your hurry
little one?

You flew into the world
on hummingbird wings

your name sings of honey
and flowers

From floppy and swaddled
to big sister kisses

To sturdy stair climber
so fast we can't follow

Wherever you walk
there is sunlight

~ Whit Humphreys ~

SNOW

Onto crust upon crust-layered snow,
buoyant, slow, cold drifting prisms
wait for north winds to blow
to end their desultory, downy settling.

Falling snow bestows its own deep silence,
as the north still holds its drifting winds closed
in icy blue rooms. Chill hounds
aching to howl through hearts and houses.

In that world stripped sound I heard,
as if by blue-numb lips murmured,
something susurrous, other,
as if I was being lured by the voice
of place penetrating self.

My breath frozen against the window warned
of isolation and a white hypnosis
by the all beautiful flakes, like stories,
told once, fused in the short memory of ice.

I am melt-water held in brief abeyance of flow.
My crystalline story will melt and unfold,
my winter become vernal freshet.
Then melt me, pond me, stock me with peepers and fish.

~ Leo Goyette ~

LOUIS

I am an only son, the eldest of three. My childhood was average by many measures. My mother stayed home and raised us while my father, who never finished high school, held a blue-collar job.

I have always felt alone. Not lonely, mind you, but alone, as though something was missing. I struggled to fill that void throughout my life, yet none of my friends, mentors or coworkers made me feel whole. I am happily married to a wonderful, kind, thoughtful woman and have three exceptional children, yet the loneliness remains. I have often wondered if that "missing something" is my twin brother.

When I consider the possibility of a brother in my mind's eye, we were fraternal twins, to ensure I would have my own identity as opposed to being "one of the twins." Naturally, we would share our father's blue eyes and wavy black hair. His name would have been Louis, after my great-grandfather.

I am left-handed. Some studies have concluded that left-handed people use the creative side of their brain more than most, which may explain why I preferred reading or playing guitar over sports, to my father's chagrin.

My dad was not athletic except in his memories. The only sport he pursued as an adult was bowling, yet to this day he regales any and all with tales of quarterbacking a neighborhood football team while in grammar school. Like many parents, he wished his only son would be the athlete he dreamt of being. On many occasions he made it clear I did not meet his athletic expectations, to the point of disparagement. Louis would have been the athlete, allowing my father to vicariously live through him and sparing me quite a bit of childhood angst.

Louis would have helped me with sports and I, being the smart one, would have helped him with homework. I would treasure the memory of the two of us playing catch in the yard until suppertime, after doing (most of) our homework.

There were two large oak trees in the backyard of my childhood home, and I built a treehouse straddling them. I can only imagine the trouble we'd get into up there, making fun of passersby, or perhaps coughing uncontrollably from our first cigarette. My mother once nearly had a heart attack when she saw me leap out of the treehouse and use a branch to safely lower myself to the ground. I can still see her on the back porch, clutching her robe with one hand while waving at me with the other, yelling for me to stop. Louis would either have reassured her it was safe, that we did it all the time, or more likely stoked her fear with stories of near-death tumbles to an unyielding earth.

We would spend a lot of time wrestling in the house until we were separated. Untold numbers of lamps and vases would have met their untimely end as one of us tumbled into them, only to blame the other during the inevitable parental confrontation. Our parents would quickly learn that sending us to our room only resulted in more chaos, so I imagine we would have spent a lot of time on opposite sides of the living room, sticking out our tongues at each other while our sisters chortled with delight.

I suspect we would have harassed and tormented our sisters whenever possible. I am responsible for a fair amount of that on my own, so I can only imagine the damage two of us could have playfully inflicted.

We would have taken on all comers in two-on-two basketball. I was not overly athletic, as I mentioned, but my "back-to-the-basket" moves were pretty good for my age (my father's opinion notwithstanding), and my brother would have possessed a devastating three-point shot. Our playground exploits would be the stuff of legend, at least when we would later tell the story.

Having a driver's license and a car meant freedom when I was 16, and we could not wait to get ours. My first car was a blue 1968 Pontiac Tempest convertible well beyond its prime. Louis would have gotten a two-door Jeep with a canvas top. Our driveway would double as an auto repair yard, much to our mother's dismay. Louis and I would work together on our cars, and our father, who worked as an auto mechanic during his teenage years, would help us with some of the more complicated repairs, reminding us to take it easy on our aging vehicles. Sharing a knowing wink or smile, we would promise to do so with no such intention. My brother would have been jealous of my convertible while I would have envied his four-wheel drive.

I would have been his wingman, and he mine. He would have charmed the ladies with his good looks and winning smile while I would have made them laugh. We would have double-dated throughout high school, taking turns driving so the other could have the back seat. I can imagine us negotiating who pays for gas and who drives. There were still a few drive-ins around back then, so they would become our dating destination of choice.

My mother married soon after she graduated high school. She often encouraged my sisters and me to attend college. When the time came, however, I realized she meant I was free to attend any school I could afford, because my parents would not pay for it. Perhaps their lack of commitment allowed me to drop out of college and pursue my dream of becoming a rock star, but that is likely just a poor excuse.

In retrospect, I was neither talented nor dedicated enough to succeed as a musician, but I was 17 and there was no one to tell me otherwise. I like to think my brother would have smacked me on the back of the head and said something like "Are you nuts? Go back to school!" On the other hand, he might have said "Hang in there, you can do it. I believe in you."

It's also possible I would have convinced him to run away and join a band with me. The thrill of striking out on our own, the sense of adventure, and the prospect of groupies may have been enough to sway him (we were teenagers after all). What young man could resist the opportunity to be part of the next Van Halen!

We would have mourned together when our younger sister died unexpectedly during her first year of college. My parents were devastated. None of us knew how to deal with such an unexpected tragedy. It took a long time for us to recover individually, and as a family.

How does a child console his parents? I vividly remember the agony I felt as I held my mother while she sobbed in my arms. I struggled to convince her that the pain of our loss would fade with time and to reassure her that the memory of her daughter would not. I wonder if I would have also had to support Louis, if he might have felt the loss even more deeply than I did.

The first woman I married was all wrong for me. With the benefit of hindsight, I understand why our marriage could not succeed, but like many young men in their twenties, I had no idea what true love was. What I saw was a pretty girl on my arm who wanted to marry me. Apparently, everyone else knew she was wrong for me, but no one wanted to say so (until after I was divorced). I believe my brother would have told me I was making a mistake in no uncertain terms.

I can be stubborn, so assuming I remained firm in my conviction to marry my first wife I am certain my brother would have set his misgivings aside and thrown me a raucous bachelor party. Our father would have attended, over our mother's objection, and we would probably still remember much of it today. This was before the advent of smartphones so there would be no mortifying off-key karaoke video to embarrass us during the holidays, much to my sister's regret.

Louis would have been there when my first child was born. He would have been her godfather and spoiled her through the years, over her mother's pro-forma objections. I am quite certain all my children would have loved their Uncle Louie. I imagine them at the window holding their baseball gloves, eagerly awaiting his arrival to play catch in the yard.

Louis would have been there when our mother died. We could have shared the burden of holding what remained of our shattered family together as we mourned the loss of the most important woman in our lives.

My father has his flaws, as do we all, but he loved my mother dearly. Helping him cope with her death was extraordinarily difficult. How do you convince someone that life goes on after he has lost a child, and now the love of his life? Perhaps Louis could have found a better way to explain why he should continue living when life seemed so cruel. Maybe he could have found a way to dry my sister's tears after she lost someone who was not only her mother, but also her best friend and confidant.

Louis would have been there for me when my marriage fell apart. He would have supported me and helped me move past what might have been the most painful chapter in my life. He would have helped me see that there was no way to save a marriage when your vain, self-centered spouse's only desires are the attention of men and spending money.

When I finally received my Computer Science degree after many years of night classes, Louis would be the first to congratulate me, and the first to remind me I should have stayed in school in the first place. We would have celebrated long into the night.

When I introduced him to the woman who would become my second wife, he would have been thrilled to know I had finally found someone to share my life with, whose humility stood in stark contrast to my first wife's vanity, and whose love of family matched my own. I would unsuccessfully admonish him not to tell tales about my first wife, and certainly not use the nickname he had given her during the divorce.

When Louis got married, I would have been his best man. When he got cold feet before his wedding, I'd remind him he was marrying the right woman for the right reasons, a woman who loved him and whose kindness and values reflected those of our mother.

Our families would spend a lot of time together, vacation together, and our children would play together. We'd compete to see who was "king of the barbeque," each trying to top the other. We would, of course, place our wives in the unenviable position of deciding whether my Kansas-City-style ribs or his "world famous" barbeque chicken was better. Being intelligent women, our wives would declare the contest a draw every time.

It was not meant to be. When I was in my 20s, my parents, to whom I had never expressed these feelings, informed me that while pregnant with me, my mother nearly miscarried. In fact, she thought she had miscarried.

Researchers estimate between 12 and 30 percent of twin pregnancies suffer from "Vanishing Twin Syndrome," where one of a set of twins does not survive the pregnancy. The causes are mostly unknown, but it is most likely provoked by fetal distress. The reported symptoms mirror my mother's.

It has also been suggested that the surviving twin in many of these cases is left-handed.

In my romanticized version of events, my brother sacrificed his life for mine.

I love and miss you, my brother.

~ Masha Harris ~

OVERDOSE

When he shows up you decide not to tell him
About the sixty milligrams of morphine you've already taken
Snorted over the course of the afternoon
A thirty here
And, when that was not enough,
A thirty there as well.
You stare at the pills in his hand as he tells you what he's brought
But you can't quite catch it
The names of the drugs, the milligrams,
A voice in your head tells you that you need to know this
It's important
But it slips between your fingertips.
Then, you know, the water, the lighter, the spoon
Scorch marks on a vinyl tablecloth burning through to the wood below
He unwraps a new needle—you told him you wanted your own
But then he shoots himself up first, so you're sharing needles again.
He apologizes, but you know he's not sorry.

You taste chemicals when the needle finds your vein
The nape of your neck burns
And you dash to the kitchen sink
Where you retch up the bile that passes for your stomach contents these days.
On the way to his friend's house he has to stop twice
So you can vomit on the side of the road
And when you get there you're so embarrassed
Because you can't keep your eyes open.
On the way back you notice the increasing panic in his voice
As he asks you, over and over again, if you're awake.

Back home you realize
You're pretty sure you're going to die tonight.
This triggers something deep inside you
And then you are weeping, weeping.
This is not his problem
And he is gone.
You go downstairs and find a razorblade
But when you get back to your room you are just so sleepy
And your breathing is shallow, shallow, shallow
And you cannot keep your eyes open
And you fall into it.

The doctors don't sugarcoat it.
There is no "You could have died,"
No "You're lucky to be alive."
There is simply,
"You should be dead."

I am

Twelve years
Three months
And twenty-nine days clean.

~ Monica Shah ~

WAITING FOR LIGHT

The morning opens purple
soft like a bruise.
I miss summer already—
the tall red oaks, patient
talismans of wonder.
Moose crossings, inky blueberries,
the dark sea, jasper stone beaches,
dusted with glittering sand.
Pine and fir forests watchful and still,
an umbrella of stars—
I am drunk with the divine.
My eyes crave emerald, olive, smoky sage.
You loved the woods,
even the forest where we found
a broken skull.
You gave me a meditation candle
on my birthday
both of us open to the world.
Now just me, waiting—
waiting to receive light.

~ Celi Byer ~

DRIFTWOOD

    I circle the shores of Lake Faye to pick up the town's trash. This morning I find aluminum foil, a child's red mitten, used hand warmers, a Cheetos wrapper, shot containers, and a plastic knife. My family scattered Dad's ashes in this water nine years ago, and in place of offering flowers or lighting candles I honor my dad by cleaning the lake.
    I wish I could stay out here forever—but the sun arcs high and I know it's time to leave Lake Faye, the skipping stones, and willows. I knot the garbage bag closed and load it into my old truck before heading to work. The drive isn't nice; Holden Bar is on the other side of I-25 in the nosy, rundown part of town. When I swing into the small lot, riddled with potholes, Mr. Adrean Mescott's already there. He joins me at the door as I turn the lock and flip the sign to OPEN. Christmas lights tinkle like shiny water in the windows even though it's late October; we keep the lights strung all year long.
    Mr. Mescott takes his seat at the counter, swivels on the stool twice, then says to me, "I got *bad* news today, Zo." He has light brown skin and gold-rimmed glasses and is always wiggling his eyebrows, asking impossible questions about stars and space. Somehow pouring drinks for him feels normal,

even though he was my high school physics teacher once. After airing the *Challenger* explosion live to my class, he got drunk during the school day and was fired.

I fix his whiskey and start to ask if his son is okay. Before I can finish the question, he elaborates, "It's not about Ollie this time. Though the news comes from him. He says some big corporation is chopping Elwick Forest. Down completely. The whole forest. For an outlet mall. Mr. Mayor just signed off on it."

My hand freezes mid-air as I'm passing Mr. Mescott his glass. "Mayor Graham? Bastard! Chopping? What gives them the right?" I think of the narrowleaf willows and pine that wrap around Lake Faye. Elwick is a beautiful, old place where kids make slingshots, teenagers relentlessly carve initials and hearts, and adults find solitude hiking the winding trails.

"They bought the plot," he says, reaching for the glass.

"It's not like it's property."

"That's exactly what it is. A piece of paper out there sure says the forest is theirs. So they got the money then the rights to knock these trees. Down."

"I never thought about it in those terms," I say. I tell him about the treehouse my dad built years ago. Getting a permit to build on public land never occurred to him. It was everybody's forest. "You're telling me they're tearing it down for a shopping center?"

"I'm afraid so. Lose the lake, lose the forest. The whole town's gonna be like. Castle Rock."

"You said 'lose the lake.' What's the lake got to do with any of this?"

Mr. Mescott proceeds to explain the repercussions of a clear-cut. Images flood my mind. I see outlets selling their discontinued crap and surplus of cheap knock-offs. I picture new housing developments choking Lake Faye's perimeter, junk piling in never-before-seen quantities, ornamental trees and invasive species, laundromat pollution, and waste turning the water to muck... He really paints a scene.

While we're talking, the door jingles and a young man I vaguely recognize slips in. "Hey, Zoey," he says, taking a seat a few chairs down from Mr. Mescott. Usually we're lax about carding but I ask for his ID because he knows my name and I forgot his.

"It's been a hot sec, Peter," I say, handing back his driver's license. Peter Robinson, the priest's nephew. I can't believe he's 21 now. Poor guy, he looks wilted; there's nothing all that remarkable about him except for a tugging weariness. He seems like he wants to be left alone, so I serve up his drink and let him sit in peace. Others come in after him. I fill and refill everyone's glasses distractedly, still engrossed in my conversation with Mr. Mescott.

Eventually, Mr. Mescott loses patience with me. "Zo. Zoey. You can give me shots, but don't go shooting the messenger."

"I wasn't trying to—"

"Mhmm. I don't know what else to tell you. I tell the truth. Scout's honor." He crosses his heart. "They *are* hacking Elwick Forest down. Shaza! Construction starts in... Oh, five months. February."

"Maybe Ollie got bad intel," I suggest.

"Not likely. It's that Coaster Bruce girl who told him. She's always up in everyone's business, you know?"

Then Elton John's "Healing Hands" comes on and Mr. Mescott takes his leave, declaring, "I *like* this song. Watch—I bet you I can get everybody up." He downs his drink, licks his teeth, and points his finger at me twice. Sure enough, he raises the room in song, arms swinging like a conductor. Adrean Mescott is just like that. He has a small crowd of lonely, mostly middle-aged men and women dancing, singing in unison. I leave a shot for him at the counter.

    I turn to Peter Robinson, one of the only people still sitting down. When he stands to go, I ask if he's good to drive. Peter's face screws up into a toothy grin and he looks like the kid I remember. "I'm good. Hey, thanks for the drinks." I reach for his empty glass after he's out the door but my hand passes through air. All that remains is a sweaty ring.

    Holden Bar finally closes for the night, and I trudge upstairs to the flat above the bar that I share with Noel. I feel like talking but there's no one to talk to. My best friend's finishing up her degree in California. Mom is like a ghost. I'm not sure she'll ever get over losing Dad. My sister's just a kid. All I've got is Noel and he won't be home until tomorrow morning. He leaves more and more often for these weekday trips, traveling all around the country. Because he owns Holden Bar, Noel can delegate work (to me, his lucky girlfriend) and take time off. Sometimes he calls these trips "research." Usually he tries to convince me to come along. But I like sticking around town.

* * *

    Here's what happened.

    Seventeen-year-old Peter Robinson left the bar drunk, turned south—away from town—and crashed his car against a guardrail. The police found him around his steering wheel, alcohol in his system, spitting distance from Holden Bar, a glass that read HOLDEN BAR intact among the wreckage, and a fake ID in his wallet.

"Oh my God, I can't believe he's... *dead*," I say to Noel once the police leave. I sat on my hands while Noel answered their questions and now they're stinging numb. "He was only seventeen?"

"The priest's nephew," Noel says and curses. "Figures he'd have a fake. I can't believe you bought that. Didn't you recognize him?"

I reel back at Noel's words. He defended me and the bar when the police came, saying we did our due diligence.

"I... You think this is my fault? I didn't remember him or how old he was, and I swear I checked the ID. It was real. I mean it looked real."

"Okay, so you checked his ID. But why didn't you try to stop him, take his keys? He must have been stumbling or slurring or something."

"What? Noel, I swear he was fine." I finally pull my hands out from under my thighs. I can't feel them at all. Still I reach for his forearm. "Look, I asked him. He said he was fine. He hardly drank a thing. I guess maybe I should've—" my voice cracks. "Is this my fault?"

"It's—This kind of thing blows over. It's fine—It's just—" Noel gets uncomfortable when I cry. He pulls his arm away and drags a hand through his carefully styled hair. A squint yanks his eyes narrow. His face is white as paper. "If I had energy for this..."

Guilt swats at my skull, then seizes like a metal band around my head. I can't think straight. I lose five pounds over the next week. Every night I zone out, staring at the bar stool where Peter drank. Noel and I don't talk about it. He tells me to just let it go and focus on work. I can't.

The incident doesn't blow over like Noel said it would. A chapter of MADD, Mothers Against Drunk Driving, opens up in Holden. Matilda Robinson, Peter's mother, spearheads the movement and files a lawsuit. The first thing MADD does is stake a white cross at the crash site to commemorate Peter. It's barely visible from Holden Bar's parking lot, a tiny white horrible dot that I can't ignore.

At first, Noel doesn't take MADD seriously. He calls the cross pathetic and laughs them off. "What do they think it is? 1920?"

But the lawsuit looms, and the MADD campaigns are relentless. Basically every woman from St. Thomas has joined. They crack down on their sons and their husbands. They start Project Red Ribbon as an awareness campaign: Tie a red ribbon on your car to remind the world that you can't drink and drive. The little triangles fly around town, flapping loudly for such small slices of fabric.

"Just say it, Noel. Just say it already," I snap when I can't take his stonewalling and sulking any longer. We lie in our bed facing away from each other. "You blame me. I know you do."

"I don't—It's not—I thought I could trust you to take care of things while I was gone," he says. "I don't understand. Why not take his keys and have someone give him a ride? I checked the receipt. Five glasses, and you really didn't notice him stumbling?"

"That's because *he wasn't stumbling*."

"You said he barely drank a thing. You weren't paying attention."

"You weren't even here! You left me to run the bar alone, *again*, so yes—maybe I was a little distracted. Mr. Mescott was telling me about the outlets and I'm worried about things changing. Worried about the lake, Noel. But I would've seen if he was stumbling or slurring. I asked and Peter said he was okay. What was I supposed to do? Hurl his keys into the snow?"

Maybe if Noel absolved me, I could stop blaming myself. But all he says is, "It's always about that lake with you."

The lake is how Noel and I met. I was circling Lake Faye, picking up trash, like I've been doing for years. Noel followed after me with bait and a fishing pole. "I've been out here all weekend, catching nothing," he said. "That water's rough as hell. Then you show up, and look how gentle the water is. This lake loves you."

Six years later and we're still together. He stood by me during the toughest times, in the wake of Dad's death. I know how he rips through places and hobbies. This year alone he's been to seven different states. He's tried out ice fishing, skiing, gardening, beekeeping, woodworking, hockey, screenwriting, and so much more. I know how much he wants to touch the skin of the world. I've fallen in love with the image of our toothbrushes clinking in the sink cup. The fresh flowers in his vintage vase. The ugly shag carpet warming his flat. And I know this bar, started by his father back in the day, means everything to him. So I promise to Noel's turned back, "I'm going to fix this."

Project Red Ribbon only does so much damage. But then, after many town hall meetings, MADD has police cars stationed around Holden. As if that weren't bad enough, members of MADD start passing out leaflets. They crowd the bar's entrance. From the window, I can make out the felt buckle hat of Matilda Robinson, black as a pupil.

"Zoey!" Mr. Mescott calls as he shoves through the door. He looks bewildered, solemn, pissed off. "While I appreciate being harassed about my age—'How old are you? How old are you anyways? Are you old enough to be here?' they asked me. Me!—Twenty-nine years old plus another thirteen! While I appreciate that, I don't like *this* one bit." He passes me a leaflet no larger than a postcard. It reads: "ALCOHOL KILLED MY FAMILY. WHAT WILL IT DO TO YOURS?" A picture of a young Peter stares out at the viewer. I'm filled with the feeling of *deadness*. The tree this paper comes from, dead. Peter, dead. My hands, ghosting.

Noel walks up from behind me and snatches the paper. I'm glad to be free of it. "Pestering like a flock of mad geese," he mutters.

"I'm no businessman, Noel," Mr. Mescott says. "The red flags whipping were one thing. Them harassing everybody walking in is another. And the police! They're making me, the Black man in the room, real nervous, Noel. Lining the road like ants. You're nearing the red."

"I hear you, Adrean."

"Did Rudy tell you he got towed last night?" When Noel shakes his head, Mr. Mescott continues. "Matilda Robinson's good friend runs Fancy Fox where we all park. Well, they've got a private company booting cars. Towing. You need a new lot. No—you need to figure something out or you won't need a lot at all."

"Yeah? How about I make prints with the words 'IT'S NOT GODDAMN 1920.' How about that? We'll call ourselves DAMM: Drunks Against Mad Mothers."

"Cheers," I say and laugh though something gnaws at my throat. Peter looks so young in that photo.

I've managed to wreck everything and I haven't worked here a full year. Before I came along, everything was all right. Money was easy. "That's the beauty of this work," Noel told me once. "It's stable. We'll never shut down. The alcohol industry's resistant to economic downturn. We th-*rived* in '81, '82. The whole country flushed down the tank but, hell, we were having fun!"

The combined force of newspaper articles, pestering at the entrance, and breathalyzer tests tanks the bar's profit. People switch to Vesper, a younger bar.

***

I have the worst dreams.

Last night I killed Peter Robinson. I wake up, and I've still gotten him killed. I know it's a bad idea but I do it anyway. I have to. I should've gone a while ago. I seek out Matilda Robinson at St. Thomas's noon service.

Low ceilings with red lights and hot, dry air... I remember this church. I practically grew up in the front pew. Everything changed when Dad died. We stopped going to service. To this day, Mom leaves the house only for mail, the night shift, groceries, and mandatory school events for my sister.

I can't focus on the priest's words. I look at Matilda's black felt hat bobbing as she nods along. I look at bloody Jesus bolted to a cross bolted to the church's wall. When it's time to approach the altar for communion, I stand up only to sit back down. Father concludes the service—"Go in peace," he says—and I approach Matilda. The aisle seems to stretch for miles. Before I close the distance, she sees me. She looks like a winter crow: beady eyes, vintage hat, and feather coat.

"Mrs. Robinson," I begin. I could have cornered her anywhere. At the market, at a MADD stakeout, at her front door. I suppose I thought she'd treat me differently in front of her God. But she shrugs her purse off her shoulder, sets it down on the pew, and plants her feet, like she's been waiting for this.

"Zoey Osmond. Your drinks killed my son four months ago and only now do you come. Well, I never—"

"Mrs. Robinson," I begin. I know it's not smart to interrupt her, especially so early in the conversation, but I can't help it. "I want you to know how sorry I am about your son," I say. "I want you to know how terrible I feel. But if you're looking for someone to punish, it's *me* you should be punishing. Not Noel. Not the bar. I—"

"That bar serves up death. You serve up death."

"We serve alcohol, Mrs. Robinson. Yes, I shouldn't have served Peter. I thought his ID was—He said he was okay to—Well, it doesn't matter. I'm sorry. I see his face all the time. I know what I have to live with. But I also see what this is doing to Noel and—"

"If you say another word about your boyfriend, so help me." "I—"

"You don't think I know that my son was struggling? He was still trying to find his way. But he was just a kid and he didn't know any better. Now he'll never go to college. He'll never be somebody's husband or somebody's father. And for what? For nothing. You waste the life God gave you, Zoey. And the worst part is you wasted my Peter's life, too."

I pause a few moments, taking a breath. This is not how I wanted things to go. Swallowing hard, I ask, "Do you remember my dad, Walter Osmond? He used to sit right there." I point to the front pew. "He would quiz us on Scripture, lead us in prayer. He burned pancakes. He paid bills. You want to talk about God's gifts? Fine. His body was God's design; God's design was a stroke. God dished death. I'm just my own two hands. Peter—"

"I don't want to hear his name from your mouth. You ask me if I knew your father? Of course I did. That's how I know your father would be ashamed of you."

"My father—"

"You worship money, booze, and nature. You think you're better than everyone else because you pick up wrappers by the lake. You think *that's* honoring your father. Your father came to this church every Sunday because he knew that nature is not God. A lake is not God. God is love. My Peter knew that. My Peter was *good* and you've taken him from me."

All I can think to say is, "My father loved me. He would love me just the same now."

"Having love doesn't mean you deserve it."

I have no answer. Her words are angry and feel unfair, but her face is that of a heartbroken mother. What can I say? I deserve this. After a few beats of silence, Matilda looks down, minutely shakes her head, and continues in a numbed voice, "But that is what God teaches. We are loved though we are not deserving. I don't forgive you today." Matilda's eyes meet mine. I can see the effort it takes for her to say, "But I want to and I will forgive you, Zoey Osmond. Because I know God, and I knew your dad. Come here." I hesitate as she beckons me to follow her to the front pew. Shaken by the change in her demeanor, I kneel stiffly by her side, an arm's width away. She starts praying and asks me to pray with her. I do.

Then she starts a story. She says that when I was really young, St. Thomas didn't have much money and was falling into disrepair. Even though my dad worked at a construction site all day and had two little girls at home, he made time to fix up St. Thomas, she says. Dad was always doing things like that, making time for people and leaving none for himself. I remember when he built memorial benches in our garage, and when he built a treehouse for me and my sister. I didn't know he built these pews though.

"The ledge we kneel upon comes from your father's faith and sacrifice, Zoey. He built these pews because he devoted his life to what is good: God, family, and community. He taught me that when I was going through—Well, it was a hard time. I owe him. And I know what he would want me to say to you: Return to God. Your best self is with God. Living between your fear and His strength. Between your memory and His omniscience." I start to say something else to her, wanting her to understand Lake Faye. But Matilda holds up her hand and shakes her head. Turning away, she collects her things, and leaves.

Just now, she's given me the greatest gift you can give to a griever: a new memory.

*　*　*

"You should sell this place," I say to Noel when I get back to the bar. We're cold and sitting too quiet in a back booth, balancing the books, closed on a Friday night. We have no business. Not even Mr. Mescott shows anymore. "Maybe Matilda—Maybe we could do something different, Noel. We could start a craft store, or antique shop."

Noel fists a drying ballpoint pen. There's nothing to write in these books.

"I have good news actually. I just didn't know how to tell you."

He stares at his white steepled hands, refusing to meet my eye. Then his thin lips slice the news. "I'm opening a second location with Brighton Outlets. They were looking for local businesses alongside the chains. I just signed the contract."

"You can't be serious."

"Zoey, we're dead-ended. We've been sued. We've been beaten. This is it. This is how we get more traffic, customers that aren't small-town tainted. This is our lifeline."

"This isn't an option."

"Why not?"

"Because of the lake! Because that mall's gonna mess everything up in town and you don't wanna be part of that. You're not—"

"Zoey, look at me. Take my hands. We could get out of here, me and you. These bars could run themselves. We could make a fortune off this deal, move to Palm Beach. Trade in a tiny lake for the whole ocean."

"It's not a tiny lake; my dad's there."

"Listen to me, Zoey. Your dad is not in that lake. The deal's done."

I pull back. I lift my eyes to Noel and see straight through to the brutal end of him.

Grief ripples fresh off my heart, strong as the day I lost Dad. I flee from the bar and straight to my truck. I handle the steering wheel. The leather—cold to the touch—feels like one large dead cow heart. Look at the blue, look at the green whizzing by. Autumn inked green ash trees yellow; now the branches stick out shamefully abandoned. The leaves have died, joining summer coneflower petals. Death layers upon death.

At first I head for the church, wanting to touch the pews Dad handcrafted. But the thought of running into Matilda or one of those MADD women stops me. Instead I remember something else my father built. Something now in danger: the old treehouse.

I make for Elwick Forest. I wonder if that treehouse is still standing, if I can even find it, somewhere in the woods.

I leave the keys in the ignition and the driver's door open. Snow beating in at a slant will cover the seat. I don't care. I twist deeper and deeper until I can't hear the sound of lakewater thunking against a strong sheet of ice. I can't remember where the damn treehouse is. The quiet scurry of little animals accompanies my scattered footfalls. I'm screaming at the caution tape. I'm screaming to the Gambel oak, juniper, pinyon, star thistle, quaking aspen. I'm screaming to God. Jesus. Peter was just a child. Where do I throw my lungs? I'm nothing but the wind, the knuckling branches, the angry crack of water against rock.

Giving up, I trudge back toward my truck. That's when I stumble across the treehouse. It used to be a spaceship; now it's tiny and dilapidated. The roof caved in at some point and the windows are broken, but it's still standing. Soon, the treehouse will be bulldozed and sold as logging or wood chips. Trucked out of town. The lake water filling its roots will dry out in a different sun. They will kill this two-hundred-year-old tree in a matter of seconds.

The idea is nuts, the idea is crazy. I can't save my father, or Peter, or the lake—but I can save this treehouse. I can lay it to rest.

I try to climb up the ladder but the first rung snaps beneath me. I grab onto the branches and pull myself up, scraping my palms against the rough bark. The floor creaks but holds my weight. I pick up pieces of the roof, and toss the rotten boards over the edge. In the corner, under some planks, I uncover our treasure chest. Inside, I find frayed Polaroids of our family, pulpy marker drawings my sister and I made for God, and a crown of prickers, the flowers long dead. I close the lid then hurl the chest through the broken window and hear it crash. Then I begin ripping at the walls, yanking any piece of rotten wood that will come loose. Nail by nail, plank by plank. My hands sting and I'm sweating and cold by the time I'm done. Only the base remains. How easy to disassemble. How heavy to cart away.

Armful by armful, I lug the pieces out of Elwick. Wood fills the trunk and backseats. It took Dad a whole summer to put this structure together. It takes me a single night. By dusk—done. The boards jut out over the middle console just above the stick shift. They poke out at uneven lengths, the top boards reaching farther than the bottom. The old wood rushes toward the windshield like a white cap.

Wood fills the trunk and backseats. It took Dad a whole summer to put this structure together. It takes me a single night. By dusk—done. The boards jut out over the middle console just above the stick shift. They poke out at uneven lengths, the top boards reaching farther than the bottom. The old, soft wood rushes toward the windshield like a white cap.

I drive to the lake. I keep the broken rung, thinking about how Dad cut, sanded, and nailed it a decade ago. The rest of the wood I set adrift in prayer.

~ Candelin Wahl ~

ENDINGS: FIVE HAIKU

three-deep cereal mix
hiking friend's bowl
before Alzheimer's

flame-red sumacs
no one oohs and ahs
waiting for maples

one mature tree
escaped the chainsaws
new parkway opens

flyover geese honk
chickadees flit
going nowhere

chilled November lawn
pouffy petticoat
last dandelion

AUTHOR BIOGRAPHIES

A lifelong New Englander, **Jeff Bernstein** would most have liked to have been, like Thoreau, "an inspector of snow-storms and rain-storms... [a] surveyor, if not of highways, then of forest paths and all across-lot routes." He is the author of two chapbooks and two full-length collections; his most recent, *The Ancient Ways*, was published in 2024 by Aldrich Press.

Celi Byer is originally from Syracuse, New York. She graduated from Emory University with a double major in Creative Writing and Environmental Science. Currently, she is a VHCB AmeriCorps member serving as the Community Engagement Coordinator at Middlebury Area Land Trust. Celi loves hiking, reading, and playing cello.

Andy Carlo lives in Huntington, Vermont, and writes mostly about his parents, but sometimes about other things that interest him—like the forests of Vermont, sugaring, cutting firewood, and the state of the world these days. His heroes are his parents (Joyce and Don Carlo), Henry Knox, Frederick Law Olmstead, and Leon Russell. He is a husband, a father of two kids who grew up too fast, and a forester.

Miriam Edelson is a neurodivergent writer, editor, settler, and mother living in Toronto. Her literary nonfiction and personal essays have appeared in literary journals and newspapers and on CBC Radio. She is the author of *My Journey with Jake: A Memoir of Parenting and Disability* (2000), *Battle Cries: Justice for Kids with Special Needs* (2005), *The Swirl in My Burl* (essays, 2022) and editor of *Deep Roots, New Threats: Confronting the Resurgent Right* (to be published in 2026). In 2016, she earned a doctorate from the University of Toronto focused on mental health in the workplace.

Leo Goyette began writing in earnest after retiring from an engineering career designing embedded computer systems. He enjoys watching football, listening to music, and playing with his grandchildren. Leo and Cheryl, his extremely patient wife of many years, live in Alton Bay, New Hampshire.

Amy Hadley is the co-author of *Backroad Ramblings, Wayfarers' Verse*, a collaboration with fellow poet and photographer, Dennis W. Gray. She has pieces published in the *Emerald Coast Review Anthology* and *Green Mountain Writers Anthology 1*. Amy enjoys penning poetry with O Henry-ish endings and twisty short fiction. She is a musician, photographer, and multimedia artist as well. During her formative years, Amy was transplanted from Long Island, New York, to coastal Alabama. She is inspired by sun, sand, and surf, influenced by moon-shine, and enthralled by the flora and fauna that share her habitat.

Amber O'Brien Haller (cover artist) is a photographer and multi-media artist living in Westford, Vermont. Amber grew up in Potsdam, New York. After earning a B.A. in Theater at SUNY Oswego she moved to New York City, where she soon realized she'd rather be behind the camera lens than in front of it! After several years in NYC, she happily downsized to Vermont and knew immediately it was a great choice. Amber enjoys life with her husband and two teenagers, along with their beloved menagerie of animals.

Masha Harris is a writer, artist, and human services worker. She's done a lot of different things—some wiser than others—and lived in a lot of different places, but she's currently settled in Vergennes, Vermont. She has previously been published in *Potash Hill* and *Chrysalis: The Journal of Transformative Language Arts*.

Whit Humphreys came to Vermont about 35 years ago after completing the Boston Museum School program with a focus on sculpture. His early days in Vermont were spent involved with The Carving Studio and quarries surrounding West Rutland. What attracted him to Vermont was the marble, the mountains, and a unique place to make art. He now lives in Benson, restoring old barns and beating back the burdock. He began writing poetry in 2021.

Karen Kish taught high school English for 25 years in Essex Junction, Vermont. She and husband Sandy also spent 15 years teaching in Poland, Egypt, and Hungary. Now retired, Karen is writing a memoir about their international teaching adventures. She enjoys cross-country skiing, traveling, gardening, biking, and tennis.

Vermont poet **Tricia Knoll** is grateful for Burlington Writers Workshop. Knoll's work appears in national and international journals and in nine published collections. *Wild Apples* (Fernwood Press 2024) is a collection of poems about moving to Vermont from Oregon. Also published in 2024, *The Unknown Daughter* features poems by people who encounter the fictional Tomb of the Unknown Daughter. Knoll is a contributing editor to the online journal *Verse Virtual*. triciaknoll.com

Patience Merriman lives in Vermont.

Nancy Mosher lives in Barre, Vermont. She has been a health care provider and administrator, and currently does leadership coaching and consulting, as well as providing and teaching Reiki. She has been writing poems and journaling since childhood and is currently working on a historical novel about her great-grandmother. Her anthology poem, "Ursine Dreaming," was inspired by recurring dreams about bears.

Kimberley Reynolds moved her family to the Mad River Valley 20 years ago to immerse them in a life of nature and community. Kim continued to write for newspapers, journals, and magazines while nurturing her love of fiction and poetry. She received an MFA from Emerson College and has continued participating in workshops and honing her craft of poetry.

Monica Shah is an educator and writer whose work explores culture, identity, and the natural world. Her poetry has appeared in *Paterson Literary Review*, *Edison Literary Review*, *Unlost*, *Muse*, and *Kaleidoscope*, as well as in the anthologies *Bolo Bolo*, *Celestial Musings*, and *Telephone*. Monica is also the recipient of a 2025 Finalist Award in poetry from the New Jersey State Council on the Arts.

Caroline Tsui is a full-time sixth-grade teacher and part-time stand-up comedian in Burlington, Vermont. She enjoys camping, skiing, and hiking. You can follow her on Instagram or X @carolineltsui. This is her first published piece.

Candelin Wahl is a late-blooming Vermont poet & songwriter. During the COVID pandemic, she took up the practice of writing haiku and haibun. Locally, her poems have hung in trees on Burlington's Poetry Path, been illuminated in Treewild's 2025 WinterDeep experience, and popped up in shop windows for Montpelier's annual PoemCity celebration. Find her work at candelinwahl.com.

ACKNOWLEDGMENTS

The Burlington Writers Workshop recognizes the hard work and commitment of the members of our writing community, who work with one another to refine and improve their writing craft. We acknowledge our workshop leaders for encouraging the artistic process, fostering collaboration and feedback in our writing groups, and providing a rich cultural forum for the literary arts. We thank the Burlington Writers Workshop Board of Directors and Leadership Team for their dedication and service to our community of writers. Thanks and appreciation go this year's reviewers for all of their time and effort in curating the pieces included in this book.

Most especially, we appreciate the poets, writers, and cover artist who have contributed to this year's anthology. The book would not exist without you!